LIVING IN THE AGE
OF THE
RAM AND THE GOAT

DARREN THOMPSON

LIVING IN THE AGE
OF THE
RAM AND THE GOAT
THE COMING WAR
BETWEEN IRAN AND THE UNITED STATES
AS FORETOLD IN THE BOOK OF DANIEL

DEFENDER
CRANE, MO

Living in the Age of the Ram and the Goat:
The Coming War between Iran and the United States as Foretold in
the Book of Daniel
Defender Publishing House,
Crane 65633
Copyright 2011 by Darren M. Thompson
All rights reserved. Published 2011

Printed in the United States of America
11 1
ISBN: 978-0983621676

Cover design by Shim Franklin

A CIP catalog record for this book is available from the Library of
Congress.

All scripture quotations are taken from the King James Version of
the Bible.

Contents

Preface

Shortly after writing my first book, *The Fourth Day: Why the Bible is Historically Accurate*, I wanted to write a book on prophecy. I noticed in my study of the Old Testament, that the eighth chapter of the book of Daniel deserved a second look. Suppose Daniel's vision of "the ram and the goat" isn't a description of Alexander the Great's military campaign against Persia. What if it is describing a chain of events that have not occurred yet? After I completed the second chapter of *this* book, I began to write several articles about the book on ezinearticles.com.

Here is an excerpt of one of the articles I wrote (Darren Thompson, "Prophecy—The Coming War Between the United States and Iran," *Ezine Articles*, July 20, 2008, http://ezinearticles.com/?Prophecy---The-Coming-War-Between-the-United-States-and-Iran&id=1342982):

> Theologians believe the vision of the goat and the ram
> describes the rise of Alexander the Great and the defeat

of the Persian Empire at his hands. What if Daniel's vision isn't about Alexander the Great, but rather about a Greek leader that has not come to power yet? What if we are living in the age of the ram and the goat? Let's look at this vision with a new perspective, as if it hasn't happened yet.

The first part of Daniel's vision describes a ram with two horns, each horn representing a different nation. The ram was seen at the Ulai River, the modern-day Karun River in Iran. The two horns are described in verse 20 [of Daniel chapter 8]; they are the kings of Media and Persia, so in modern-day terms, who are these two countries? Persia is easy; that is Iran. Who is Media? They are a group of people that claim to be a nation yet have no land of their own. They live in Turkey, Iraq, and Iran and have been persecuted in all three of these nations. They are the people of Kurdistan: the Kurds. Therefore, the ram is an alliance of Iran and the Kurds.

So is the ram in place today? Not quite. Ahmadinejad, the present leader of Iran as of this writing, is no friend to the Kurds living in Iran. The situation will have to change on the Iranian political scene to be considered allies of Iran. However, change may be on the horizon. There are signs of vast discontent in Iran, mostly associated with Ahmadinejad's mishandling of Iran's economy and the yearning of Iran's people for political freedom. A democratic movement is gaining momentum in Iran and one of the chief political forces behind that movement is the Kurds. Therefore, I believe the ram will not be in place until political upheaval dislodges Ahmadinejad from power and Iran adopts democracy as it new form of government.

The people of Iran took to the streets in June of 2009, to demonstrate their displeasure regarding the reelection of Ahmadinejad. This was an election that the demonstrators (and much of the world as well) believed was a rigged contest. These protesters are now known as "the green movement" and are responsible for the political turmoil that Ahmadinejad continues to battle today. What you may find fascinating about the article I wrote, is that I didn't write this article after the election. In fact, I had written this article on July 20, 2008 and it was based on a chapter I had written in 2007. (As of the date of this writing, this article is still posted at ezinearticles.com.) I had posted it on ezinearticles.com eleven months before this election!

I am more than a little nervous after realizing how close my novel interpretation of Daniel chapter 8, and the recent political upheaval in Iran, have paralleled. This realization has convinced me that there is a finite period of time left for us to prepare for the coming of Christ. I am convinced that we are living during the age of the fulfillment of Daniel's vision of the ram and the goat.

Introduction

In the third year of the reign of king Belshazzar a vision appeared unto me, even unto me Daniel, after that which appeared unto me at the first. And I saw in a vision; and it came to pass, when I saw, that I was at Shushan in the palace, which is in the province of Elam; and I saw in a vision, and I was by the river of Ulai. Then I lifted up mine eyes, and saw, and, behold, there stood before the river a ram which had two horns: and the two horns were high; but one was higher than the other, and the higher came up last. I saw the ram pushing westward, and northward, and southward; so that no beasts might stand before him, neither was there any that could deliver out of his hand; but he did according to his will, and became great. And as I was considering, behold, an he goat came from the west on the face of the whole earth, and touched not the ground: and the goat had a notable horn between his eyes. And he came to the ram that had two horns, which I had seen standing before the river, and ran unto him in the fury of his power. And I saw him come close unto the ram, and he was moved with choler against him, and smote the ram, and brake his two horns: and there was no power in the ram to stand before him, but he cast him down to the ground, and stamped upon him: and there was none that could deliver the ram out of his hand. Therefore the he goat waxed very great: and when he was strong, the great horn was broken; and for it came up four notable ones toward the four winds of heaven.

DANIEL 8:1–8

Conservative scholars have interpreted the above passage as a description of historical events that occurred when Alexander the Great invaded the Persian Empire. The "ram" is symbolic of the Persian Empire, and the two horns are symbolic of the two kingdoms: the Medes and the Persians that form the Persian Empire. The "rough goat" represents the Greek Empire. How did the scholars make this symbolic comparison? They didn't. The angel (Gabriel) from Daniel's vision linked these animals with their corresponding world power: "The ram which thou sawest having two horns are the kings of Media and Persia. And the rough goat is the king of Grecia: and the great horn that is between his eyes is the first king" (Daniel 8:20–21). I believe that these scholars have made an error in the timeframe when this vision of Daniel's was to be fulfilled. This vision does not describe the events of the life of Alexander the Great, but rather events that are to occur prior to the end times, events that may occur during our lifetime. Consider the details of the following passage: "And I heard a man's voice between the banks of the Ulai, which called, and said, Gabriel, make this man to understand the vision. So he came near where I stood: and when he came, I was afraid, and fell upon my face: but he said unto me, Understand, O son of man: for at the time of the end shall be the vision" (Daniel 8:16–17).

It is clear from the phrase "at the time of the end" these events happen during the end times, the timeframe when the events of the book of Revelation begin to transpire; and for reasons that I will make apparent later, I believe this vision of the ram and the goat describes events that mark of the beginning of the end times. So let's reexamine this great vision of Daniel's in light of the events of our present age.

1

Daniel's Vision of the Ram and the Goat

The Ram as Seen in the 21st Century

Let's take a close look at the events of the vision of the ram and the goat, verse by verse:

Daniel 8:1

> **In the third year of the reign of the king Belshazzar a vision appeared unto me, even unto me Daniel, after that which appeared unto me at the first.**

Daniel indicates in this verse that this vision occurred during the "reign of Belshazzar," the third Babylonian king mentioned in the Bible after Nebuchadnezzar and Evil-Merodach (Amel-Marduk). This vision occurred after the vision that is described in Daniel chapter 7.

Daniel 8:2

> **And I saw in a vision; and it came to pass, when I saw, that I was at Shushan in the palace, which is in the province of Elam; and I saw in a vision, and I was by the river of Ulai.**

Daniel is relocated during his vision from Babylon where King Belshazzar had his capital to Shushan, the capital of the Persian Empire (Elam was part of the Persian Empire), which was led by Cyrus the Great at that time. The Persian Empire is the same geographical area as modern-day Iran. The river of Ulai is the present-day Karun River in Iran and it is located very near the Iraq/Iran border. The Karun River is historically and militarily significant, because it is the place where the militarily weaker Iranians were able to stand against Saddam Hussein's forces during the Iraq/Iran war.

Daniel 8:3

> **Then I lifted up mine eyes, and saw, and, behold, there stood before the river a ram which had two horns: and the two horns were high: but one was higher than the other, and the higher came up last.**

The two horns of the ram represent the modern-day descendants of the empires of Persia and Media. How do we know this? Again, the angel Gabriel tells us (Daniel 8:20): "The ram which thou sawest having two horns are the kings of Media and

Persia." We know that Persia represents the nation of Iran, but what nation does Media represent? The only present-day ethnic group that claims to be descendants of the nation of Media is the Kurds, the people of Kurdistan. What is ironic about Kurdistan is that presently, no one considers Kurdistan a military threat because of its unique circumstances as a nation. Kurdistan has 25 million people, yet it is a country with no official borders. The Kurdistan people live as the minority people in several different countries in an unofficial area that includes western Iran, northern Iraq, northern Syria, and eastern Turkey. The only autonomous government recognized is the federal entity that the Kurds control in Iraq. Hist orically, the Kurds have been persecuted in whatever country they inhabited, Iraq and Turkey being the worst offenders. Yet, according to this verse, they will rise as a nation to be reckoned with. Obviously in the context of modern-day events, Iran is the horn that rises first according to this verse, but Kurdistan will be the powerful nation that rises last. This description of the Kurds "being last" has two possible types of fulfillment. The first possibility is the more obvious: The Kurds rise to power in Iran after the Iranians. The second possibility is more subtle: The Kurds are the last kingdom of the end-times scenario, the kingdom of the Antichrist. I believe both of these events will happen. Note that this verse states that the second horn will rise *last*, and not *second* or *next*. This is an important distinction as well as an important clue. I believe that this indicates that the "little horn" of the Antichrist that will rise in Daniel 8:9 is the last nation that will rise in the end times: Kurdistan. One day, Kurdistan will have its own borders, its own government, and will be a world power.

How close is the ram to being unified? I will refer back to the article I wrote on ezinearticles.com, *Prophecy—The Coming War Between the United States and Iran*, in July 2008, about the unification of the Kurds with Iran's political system. I described in the article that the Kurds are being oppressed in Iran like much of its other citizens, and has been a major political force in the grassroots democracy movement in Iran. The only way you can consider the Kurds and Iran to be unified is if there is a dramatic change in the Iranian political system. Here is how I described that change: "A democratic movement is gaining momentum in Iran and the chief political force behind the movement is the Kurds. Therefore, I believe the ram will not be in place until political upheaval dislodges Ahmadinejad from power and Iran adopts democracy as its new form of government."

I wrote this about eleven months prior to the controversial election results that occurred in Iran in June 2009, which initiated the "green movement" (democracy movement) in Iran. I do not believe that Iran will transform into a true democracy. It can only be considered a union of the hardliners in Iran and the democratic movement of the Kurds if the government is a compromise of an Islamic theocratic dictatorship that has given in to the demands of the democratic movement in order to retain its political power. A major plank of the democratic movement is to stop the push for nuclear weapons that is currently being advocated for in Iran and are not really advocates for any military campaign. It will be the hardliners and their aspirations that will make Iran a great power in the Middle East and will cause the ram to control the Persian Gulf nations as we will see next.

Daniel 8:4

> **I saw the ram pushing westward, and northward, and southward; so that no beasts might stand before him, neither was there any that could deliver out of his hand; but he did according to his will, and became great.**

According to this verse, the ram (the nations of Iran and Kurdistan) will first push westward, then it will push northward, and then southward.

The word "push" in this verse literally means to "gore" as in the goring caused by a horned animal. Symbolically, it is used in other places in the Bible to indicate the expansion of a nation. Therefore, according to this verse, Iran will expand westward, northward, and southward. What countries might be conquered by Iran and Kurdistan if this is true? It is interesting to note that this verse indicates that Iran will invade to the west, then the north, and finally to the south. I think this pattern of conquest reveals Iran's future objectives. Since Iraq is Iran's largest military opponent in the region and it is located to the west of Iran, it only makes sense that Iran would conquer Iraq first, thus invading westward. Once Iran has conquered Iraq, it would invade Turkey (northward) and Saudi Arabia (southward), thus it will have conquered the most powerful nations in the Persian Gulf area. An additional possibility is that it could also invade the Caspian Sea region since it is north of Iraq.

Why Invade the Caspian Sea?

When the Soviet Union ceased to exist and broke up into smaller countries in the early 1990s, the United States and Europe saw an opportunity to increase the security of the worldwide oil supply. There was evidence that the Caspian Sea had vast potential as a new source of petroleum, but it had not been developed because the Soviet Union did not have the resources to expand the infrastructure necessary to drill and transport the oil. When the Soviet Union was still in power, the only nations on the coast of the Caspian Sea were the Soviet Union and Iran. However, after the Soviet Union's fall from power, new, smaller nations appeared on the coast of the Caspian Sea from the former Soviet Union: Turkmenistan, Armenia, Georgia, and Azerbaijan.

The United States and Europe began to invest heavily in these new countries to develop the petroleum resources in the Caspian Sea with the hope that they would be friendlier than the Soviet Union or Iran. Presently, the Caspian Sea only accounts for 3 percent of the world's oil supply, but it has been speculated it may have as much as 25 percent of the world's oil supply. The United States and Europe have also helped to finance the BTC (Baku-Tblisi-Ceyhan) pipeline that runs through Azerbaijan, Georgia, and Turkey on the west side of the Caspian Sea near Iraq that transports oil to the Mediterranean Sea. These activities by the United States and Europe have not gone unnoticed by Russia and Iran, who consider the Caspian Sea "their backyard."

Rumors abound that the Russians have tried unsuccessfully to sabotage the BTC pipeline. If Iran controlled this pipeline, it could achieve its goal of removing the influence of the United States and Europe from the Caspian Sea, but it could also drastically increase the worldwide price of petroleum; a move that would benefit their national economy. They could easily control the pipeline by successfully invading Turkey. Iran then would have complete control of over two-thirds of the world's oil resources since it would control the Caspian Sea and the Persian Gulf. As it written in Daniel 8:4, Iran would indeed be "great."

Why Would Iran Invade Turkey, Saudi Arabia, and Iraq?

The possibility that Iran could invade Turkey and Saudi Arabia is certainly disturbing, but how likely is this to happen? What motivation would Iran have to do this? This military action would be consistent with Iran's goals for the Muslim world. Iran's objective is to be the leader of the Muslim nations in the Middle East. Their strategy is to "flip" those countries that are allies of the U.S. to Islamic theocracies that are supportive of Iran. Turkey, Saudi Arabia, and Iraq are all allies of the U.S., and Iran's ultimate goal is to remove any influence that the U.S. has in the region.

Can Iran defeat Turkey, Saudi Arabia, and Iraq militarily? I found that globalfirepower.com is a very useful Web site that can help answer this question. This Web site collects information about the different aspects of individual nations and ranks them in order of their military strength. According to globalfirepower.com, Iran should certainly be able to handle

Iraq or Saudi Arabia in a military conflict, since Iran is ranked #18, while Iraq is ranked #37, and Saudi Arabia is ranked #24. When you look at the details of these countries' military, the amount of military hardware is comparable between each of them. However, what would appear to be the big difference is the size of Iran's manpower; Iran has nine times more active military personnel and reserves than either Saudi Arabia or Iraq. Invading Turkey successfully will be more difficult.

According to the Web site, Turkey is ranked #10 while Iran is ranked #18. The active military and reserves are essentially equivalent for the two nations. When you analyze both countries' military hardware, Turkey is much more dominant in their air based weapons (1,199 for Turkey and eighty-four for Iran). This is primarily due to the fact that Turkey has its own F-16 factory that it uses to manufacture jet fighters for itself and NATO. What may set Iran apart is its paramilitary force. Iran claims to have a paramilitary force of over 12 million, the largest paramilitary force in the world. If Iran does use this 12-million-soldier paramilitary as its major invading force, it does explain the biblical description of the movement of its invasion. As I mentioned previously, Iran goes West (to Iraq), then North (to Turkey), and then south (to Saudi Arabia). Since Iran doesn't have the naval resources to move a 12-million-man group across the Persian Gulf, this force will have to walk to Saudi Arabia. This means they will have to go west into Iraq first, and then walk south (around the Persian Gulf) to get to Saudi Arabia. Iran employed this paramilitary group effectively during the Iran/Iraq war by using them to clear minefields so that their "regular" forces could march unimpeded into Iraq.

Military analysts in the United States have questioned whether Iran can actually have a 12-million-man paramilitary, since they only trained 2 million for the Iraq/Iran war in the 1980s and only put five hundred thousand of those into battle. If Iran does indeed have that large of a paramilitary force, then Turkey's advantage in airpower may be nullified.

Iran also has another weapon: an economic weapon. According to the globalfirepower.com Web site, Turkey produces about forty-five thousand barrels of oil per year but consumes more than six hundred fifty thousand barrels per year, which means they have to import a little more than 90 percent of all their petroleum. Ironically, Russia and Iran are the two largest importers of oil to Turkey. If Iran and Russia were to conspire together (they *do* have a close political relationship) and stop oil from flowing to Turkey, that might be the easiest mechanism to invade Turkey. Alternately, Iran could invade without Russia's help. Turkey has positioned itself as the distributor of oil and natural gas from Asia to the rest of the world. According to an article written by The Washington Institute for Near East Policy (Soner Cagaptay and Nazli Gencsoy, "Startup of the Baku-Tbilisi-Ceyhan Pipeline: Turkey's Energy Role," *Washington Institute for Near East Policy*, May 27, 2005, http://www.washingtoninstitute.org/template C05.php?CID=2319), there are several pipelines for gas and oil that exist or are under consideration to deliver product from the Caspian Sea, Iraq, and Russia to the Mediterranean Sea. All these pipelines appear to go through Ceyhan, Turkey. If Iran were to capture Ceyhan and control the pipelines, that may be all that is required to force Turkey into submission.

Iran's control of Turkey, Saudi Arabia, and Iraq could also address their economic goals. Control of Iraq and Saudi Arabia would obviously increase Iran's control of the world oil supply, but it would also give them something they desperately need for Iran: more refinery capacity. Iran ships much of its oil unrefined since it doesn't have much refinery capacity. According to nationmaster.com (a Web site that collects economic statistical information about countries), Saudi Arabia and United Arab Emirates (a small country located alongside Saudi Arabia on the Persian Gulf Coast) are ranked #8 and #7 among nations that produced refined oil. Together, they have twenty times more oil refining capacity than Iran. It makes sense that as Iran invades to the south they would invade Saudi Arabia and the United Arab Emirates together for their refining capability.

This invasion also helps Iran in controlling distribution of their oil supply. According to geographic.org, Iran currently has the eighteenth largest tanker capacity in the world. When the tankers of Iran, Turkey, and Saudi Arabia are combined after Iran's invasion, Iran would have the fifth largest tanker capacity of any country. As I have mentioned already, Iran's control of Turkey would mean they would also control the oil that comes through the pipelines from the Caspian Sea, Russia, and Iraq and consequently gas or oil going to Europe. Controlling Turkey means that Iran would also control the Straits of Bosporuss and the Dardanelles that are the sea lanes into the Black Sea. According to the previously mentioned Washington Institute article, over five thousand tankers carrying Caspian Sea oil pass through these Straits every year and the Black Sea is the location of Russia's main shipping port.

Not only is it possible that there could be an Iranian invasion of these Persian Gulf countries, but there is one report that endorses this as a likely scenario. An internet magazine called "DEBKA-Net-Weekly" has referenced a report by Army General Ray Odierno describing the impact of American forces finally leaving Iraq (Unknown Author, "Hizballah's Nasrallah Lights a Fire," *Debka-Net-Weekly*, Vol.10, Issue 456, pp. 6–8, August 6, 2010, http://www.debka.com/weekly/456/). This report is an "unvarnished prognosis of complete political and security chaos in Baghdad, armed conflicts between Sunnis and Shiites and between Kurds, Shiites and Sunnis, and the loss of all of southern Iraq, from Basra in the south to the central region of Karbala, to an Iranian land grab." Shiite commanders in the Iraqi Army are preparing to conduct an "all-out offensive" against Sunnis in Baghdad and central and western Iraq as soon as the American forces leave. While the Shiites and Sunnis are fighting each other, it is proposed that the Kurds of Northern Iraq will solidify control of their part of the country and expand control as far south towards Baghdad as possible. Finally, the report "makes no bones about an Iranian offensive in the making to snatch the Iraq's main oilfields around the port-town of Basra, which account for 60 percent of nation oil output." Iran will also seek to seize the two holiest Shiite locations: the mass pilgrimage shrine-cities of Karbala, and Najef, south of Baghdad. Iran will be after oil and religious centers. It is clear that U.S. intelligence experts expect, at the very least, an Iranian invasion of Iraq.

Enter the Goat

Daniel 8:5a

And as I was considering, behold, an he goat came from the west on the face of the whole earth, and touched not the ground...

Many theologians believe that Daniel 8:5 describes the military campaign of Alexander the Great. They argue that Alexander's invasion covered the face of the "known" world as the Bible viewed it, and that the Bible is using the phrase "touched not the ground" as a poetic reference to the speed of Alexander's forces (in other words, Alexander's forces moved with such speed it was "like" they didn't touch the ground).

When this verse is considered describing military forces in the present age, one does not have to consider this phrase as a metaphor, but it could very well be a literal description. Wars that have involved battles in which the combatants did not touch the ground have only occurred since World War I when biplanes armed with machine guns battled one another in the sky. Airplanes began to use bombs against land and sea targets in World War II. Also, in World War II, battleships became powerful weapons from the sea with their ability to lob "Volkswagen" sized munitions at their land targets. The Vietnam War era introduced the capability of the world's superpowers to launch munitions halfway around the world using intercontinental ballistic missiles (ICBMs). If there is a time that nations have become well suited to conducting war without touching the ground, it is during our generation.

The "he goat" that "came from the west on the face of the whole earth" also refers to events in our generation. If the he goat comes from the west and is a "group" that consists of every nation from "the face of the whole earth," then doesn't this sound like a description of the United Nations? The United Nations headquarters is located in New York City which is certainly to the west of the events described here. This interpretation would not contradict this phrase and it is also descriptive of a scenario that is possible in our lifetime: the Secretary General of the United Nations could use a multinational force against Iran and the Kurds. Therefore, if the Secretary General is the he goat, he must also represent the nation of Greece as stated previously. So, this prophecy can only occur sometime in our future when the Secretary General of the United Nations is from Greece. Is this a possibility?

The United Nations selected a new Secretary General, Ban Ki-moon (the South Korean candidate) who began his term in office in January 2007. A great deal of political arm twisting normally takes place in the process of selecting a Secretary General, and Ban Ki-moon's appointment was no different. China, which has the power of veto over any potential nominee, was adamant that the next candidate come from Asia. The United States, who also has the power of veto over any potential candidate, held the position that the next candidate shouldn't necessarily come from Asia, but conceded when China indicated that the candidate from South Korea, a prominent democracy in the region, was acceptable to them. This process of deciding who will be the next Secretary General is often decided based on which region has not had an opportunity to have a Secretary General in office that is from their region. Therefore, we should be able to ascertain which region the *next* Secretary General will come from based on the number of Secretary Generals that have been selected from each region. Three Secretaries General have come from Western Europe, two from Africa, one from Latin America, and, including Ban Ki-moon, two from Asia. Eastern Europe has not had any from their region yet, however, the United States did make some argument for Eastern Europe during Ban Ki-Moon's selection.

As a result, if this process is based on fairness, it would appear Eastern Europe should have a chance at Secretary General next. I think this depends on the viewpoint of the sitting president of the United States. If that president is friendlier to the European Union than these former countries of the Soviet Union (the Eastern European nations), then the selection of the Secretary General from a European Union member is very possible. Greece just happens to be a member of the European Union and it is not far removed from the countries of Eastern Europe. If Greece is selected, how soon could this occur? The Secretary General has a five-year term in office, but is limited to two terms and with few exceptions they are reappointed and serve for the full ten years. However, in the case of Ban Ki-Moon, prospects for a ten-year appointment don't look so good.

Consider this excerpt from an article from The Korea Times online (Tom Plate, "In Defense of Ban Ki Moon," *The Korea Times*, August 30, 2009, http://www.koreatimes.co.kr/www/news/opinion/2011/02/172_50925.html): "But now Ban, at the halfway mark of his five-year term, finds the prospect of the second term mysteriously up in the air." *Therefore*, it appears that the selection process for a new Secretary General of the U.N. could start as soon as 2011, and the appointment of a Secretary General of the U.N. from Greece could happen in the very near future.

President Barack Obama also seems to be making arrangements to select the next Secretary General of the United Nations in 2011. According to an article from the internet magazine Inner City Press, Obama may be in the process of making a deal with China so they will not veto his attempt to select a new Secretary General (Matthew Russell Lee, "Of UN Women and Ban Ki-Moon's Second Term, Dirty Deals, Double Crosses, Albright Boutros Echoes," *Inner City Press*, August 2, 2010, http://www.innercitypress.com/ban1second080210.html). The Obama administration does not believe it can accomplish its political goals with Ban Ki-Moon as the leader of the U.N. Inner City Press reports that the U.S. may "cede the top post at the World Bank [a position that has until now only been given to an American appointed by the U.S. President] in 2012 to China, in exchange for Asia Group control of the UN S-G post being moved, and Obama getting his own choice."

The Notable Horn

Daniel 8:5b

...and the goat had a notable horn between his eyes.

The first observation one should make when analyzing the *notable horn* is a result of the following question: Why doesn't the Bible describe the horn as a "single" horn rather than a "notable" horn? Again, many theologians have inter-preted the appearance of this he goat to be a unicorn: a goat with one horn. What if the goat actually has more than one hundred and ninety-two horns (which would look more like a porcupine than a unicorn), that represent the member nations of the United Nations, and those horns are located all over its body? What if the notable horn is striking in its appearance, relative to every other horn the he goat has, because it is a mighty military superpower, the world's only military superpower? The word "notable" is not really in context here unless it is describing the appear-ance of one unique horn compared to the other horns of the he goat.

Thus, the use of the word "notable" in this verse would be completely consistent if it is referring to a multi-horned goat with one large horn sticking out of its forehead.

Note the location of the notable horn. It is located between the eyes of the goat. Why is this important? I believe that this symbolism indicates that the notable horn has great influence over the direction of the he goat compared to the other horns: the notable horn leads the eyes of the goat in the direction he should look. Is there a country that presently fits this descrip-tion that is member of the United Nations better than the United States of America? It is obvious that the notable horn must be a representation of the United States.

Now, for the sake of clarity, let's assemble the individual parts of these observations. The he goat is the United Nations led by a Secretary General who is from the nation of Greece and the notable horn represents the United States.

The Goat and the Ram Collide

Daniel 8:6

And he came to the ram that had two horns, which I had seen standing before the river, and ran unto him in the fury of his power.

Since the United States still has a major presence in the Persian Gulf because of the Iraq and Afghanistan conflicts, something must occur for this prophecy to take place. I don't think Iran will invade Iraq as long as the United States is present in the Persian Gulf. I believe there is already movement in this regard since the United States is scheduled to leave Iraq in 2011 (General Petraeus has an agreement with President Obama to extend this to 2014, but it wouldn't surprise me if Obama reverts to the 2011 date to appease his left-wing constituents). Based on recent posturing by President Obama, we could be leaving Afghanistan by 2011 (or 2014) as well.

According to this verse, the he goat confronts the ram at the Ulai (Karun) River near the Iran/Iraq border. How is this possible since the ram "pushed westward" and presumably conquered Iraq? Well, note how the ram has been moving so far: previously the he goat didn't touch the ground (so he is presumably flying), but in this verse the he goat is running at the ram. I believe this indicates that the he goat is able to take back control of Iraq from the air, and then the he goat uses Iraq as his staging point to conduct a land war against the ram.

The Ram's Horns are Broken

Daniel 8:7–8

> And I saw him come close unto the ram, and he was moved with choler against him, and smote the ram, and brake his two horns: and there was no power in the ram to stand before him, but he cast him down to the ground, and stamped upon him: and there was none that could deliver the ram out of his hand. Therefore the he goat waxed very great: and when he was strong, the great horn was broken; and for it came up four notable ones toward the four winds of heaven.

Here the he goat is able to successfully defeat the ram and his two horns. Iran and Kurdistan are broken. While they may be broken, Iran and Kurdistan still have important roles in other end-time events.

It is interesting to note the emotional state of the goat. He is "moved with choler." This phrase is translated "filled with bitterness" in other parts of the Old Testament. We have seen in Daniel 8:6 that the goat ran at the ram in the "fury" of his power. This word "fury" means extreme anger in the original Hebrew language. The book of Jeremiah has a similar description of Iran, referred to as Elam, from the very mouth of God (Jeremiah 49:35–39):

> Thus saith the Lord of hosts; Behold, I will break the bow of Elam, the chief of their might. And upon Elam

will I bring the four winds from the four quarters of heaven, and will scatter them toward all those winds; and there shall be no nation whither the outcasts of Elam shall not come. For I will cause Elam to be dismayed before their enemies, and before them that seek their life: and I will bring evil upon them, even my fierce anger, saith the LORD; and I will send the sword after them, till I have consumed them: And I will set my throne in Elam, and will destroy from thence the king and the princes, saith the LORD. But it shall come to pass in the latter days, that I will bring again the captivity of Elam, saith the LORD.

I believe this passage in Jeremiah is describing the defeat of the ram by the goat because of several clues in the passage. The Lord has "fierce anger" toward Elam, just as the goat charges in his "fury" at the ram. When the Lord "brings the four winds from the four quarters of heaven" against Elam; couldn't this be a description of the whole world (through the U.N.) engaged in air combat with Iran? As you have probably noticed, there are several interesting details that I haven't discussed here, like the captivity of Elam. I will discuss those in chapter 3 when I talk about Daniel chapter 11.

The he goat, the Greek Secretary General of the United Nations, will become very powerful since the United Nations should have control of rebuilding the entire Persian Gulf and (possibly) the Caspian Sea after taking control of it from Iran (as I stated earlier this area should represent at least two-thirds of the world petroleum supply).

The most disturbing event in these two verses is the breaking of the great horn. Note the phrase, "when he was strong, the great horn was broken." This phrase implies that after this great military victory for the United States, the United States is somehow "broken." What is curious about this verse is that it doesn't say how the great horn is broken. It certainly could be through internal events like an economic catastrophe, or a political struggle, or even an unmentioned military struggle.

The Four Kings from the Four Directions

When the great horn is broken, four notable ones come up in its place in the direction of the four winds of heaven. What is being described here? I believe that once the U.S. is removed as the stabilizing influence in the world (the glue that holds the U.N. together), its demotion from its position as a world superpower will result in the U.N. breaking up into four "mini United Nations." These four mini U.N. organizations will represent a different part of the globe: the Americas and Europe (east direction), Russia and the Middle East (north direction), Asia (west direction), and Africa (south direction). All these directions are relative to the nation of Israel since Jerusalem is the center of the world by God's perspective. Also, there will be a notable "horn," the most influential nation in that particular region that acts as the leader for each of these respective organizations. It is important to note that one of the purposes of the United Nations is to protect weaker nations from the aggressor nations. This is only possible if there is a militarily strong nation that is the leader of the nations that is willing to conduct "police" actions when necessary, so, it is necessary for each of these organizations to have one nation that is equal in military might to the strongest nation in the other groups. What is currently interesting is that there is a strong military power in each of the four parts of the globe except for Africa. This suggests that a strong military nation will rise in Africa to cause the fulfillment of this scripture.

Does the Bible give any clues as to the identity of these four horns, these nations that will lead their respective part of the globe? I believe Daniel chapter 11 describes some of the actions of the kingdoms of the north and the south. A descendant of the daughter of the king of the south invades the land of the king of the north and brings the spoils of war home: "But out of a branch of her roots shall one stand up in his estate, which shall come with an army, and shall enter in the fortress of the king of the north, and shall deal against them, and shall prevail: And shall also carry captives into Egypt their gods, with their princes, and with their precious vessels of silver and gold; and he shall continue more years than the king of the north" (Daniel 11:7–8).

Therefore, based on this verse, the horn from the south is Egypt. In fact, Egypt is mentioned several times relative to the actions of the "king of the south" in Daniel chapter 11.

Russia is the nation from the north. This becomes very evident as we look at Daniel chapter 11 later in this book.

While the Bible is not as clear in its description of the king from the west I believe the Bible does mention this nation in several scriptures regarding the end times.

Greece is the only country mentioned by name in the Bible that is involved in end-time events that is located west of Israel (Zechariah 9:13): "When I have bent Judah for me, filled the bow with Ephraim, and raised up thy sons, O Zion, against thy sons, O Greece, and made thee as the sword of a mighty man."

God strengthens Israel in this verse to defend itself from Greece in the end times. It becomes apparent that when the United Nations splits into four different world organizations, the former Secretary General of the United Nation that represented Greece before the four-way split becomes the leader of the organization that represents the western portion of the globe (the Americas and Europe).

The Bible doesn't give any information as to the identity of the nation that represents the king of the east, although the Old Testament and New Testament do indicate that the king of the east does engage the king of the north at some point during the end times: "But tidings out of the east and out of the north shall trouble him [king of the north]; therefore he shall go forth with great fury to destroy, and utterly to make away many" (Daniel 11:44).

"And the sixth angel poured out his vial upon the great river Euphrates; and the water thereof dried up, that the way of the kings of the east might be prepared" (Revelation 16:12).

Kurdistan: The Little Horn

Daniel 8:9

> **Out of one of them came forth a little horn, which waxed exceeding great, toward the south, and toward the east and toward the pleasant land.**

As I have mentioned previously, I believe that Kurdistan is the little horn, the country that is home to the Antichrist that brings such devastation to the world in the end times. Kurdistan will be the last kingdom to rise, the only country which claims to be the descendant of the Medes (as mentioned above this is the chief requirement necessary to be the last kingdom to rise). Daniel 8:9 describes a further requirement of the little horn; it must come from one of the four horns that arise after the great horn of the he goat is broken. As we will see later, Russia will fall as the king of the north and the Antichrist will arise in Iraq (Babylon). Note that Daniel 11:23 describes the Antichrist and the fact that he will "become strong with a small people"; this certainly fits the description of the Kurds.

Summary of Daniel Chapter 8

The following is a summary of the events that I believe will fulfill the events as described by the book of Daniel, chapter 8:

1. "I saw the ram pushing westward, and northward, and southward; so that no beasts might stand before him, neither was there any that could deliver out of his hand, but he did according to his will, and became great" (verse 4). The ram represents Iran and Kurdistan (the Kurds in Iraq). Iran and Kurdistan will conquer Iraq, then the countries around the Caspian Sea and finally the countries of the Persian Gulf so that Iran and Kurdistan control the world's oil supply.

2. "As I was considering, behold, an he goat came from the west on the face of the whole earth, and touched not the ground and the goat had a notable horn between his eyes" (verse 5). The goat represents the United Nations when it is lead by a Secretary General from Greece and the notable horn represents the United States. The United Nations and the United States come against Iran and Kurdistan and defeat them. "Therefore the he goat waxed very great: and when he was strong, the great horn was broken; and for it came up four notable ones toward the four winds of heaven" (verse 8). Shortly after this victory, the United States ceases to be a military power (the Bible doesn't specify how). The United Nations divides into four smaller multinational organizations that represent the four directions (north, south, east, and west). The north will be led by Iraq, the south will be led by Egypt, and the West will be led by Greece (the Bible doesn't specify which country is the lead nation from the east).

3. "And out of one of them came forth a little horn, which waxed exceeding great, toward the south, and toward the east, and toward the pleasant land" (verse 9). The little horn, the last kingdom to rise that are the descendants of the Medes, is the nation of Kurdistan and Kurdistan will arise out of Iraq.

2

Identifying the Four Beasts of Daniel

The Dream of Nebuchadnezzar's Statue

The circumstances of the historical events that surround the life of Daniel become important during a particular dream of King Nebuchadnezzar's. One of the first tests of faith in the life of Daniel is a situation in which King Nebuchadnezzar has a dream that disturbs him greatly, yet he can't remember the details of the dream when he awakens. Therefore, he orders the wise men of his kingdom to analyze his dream, but they must also tell him the details of the dream; if they can't he is going to have all of them executed. Since Daniel is part of the group of wise men he seeks God in prayer to reveal the mystery of the king's dream (Daniel 2:28–45):

> But there is a God in heaven that revealeth secrets, and maketh known to the king Nebuchadnezzar what shall be in the latter days. Thy dream, and the visions of

thy head upon thy bed, are these; As for thee, O king, thy thoughts came into thy mind upon thy bed, what should come to pass hereafter: and he that revealeth secrets maketh known to thee what shall come to pass. But as for me, this secret is not revealed to me for any wisdom that I have more than any living, but for their sakes that shall make known the interpretation to the king, and that thou mightest know the thoughts of thy heart. Thou, O king, sawest, and behold a great image. This great image, whose brightness was excellent, stood before thee; and the form thereof was terrible. This image's head was of fine gold, his breast and his arms of silver, his belly and his thighs of brass, his legs of iron, his feet part of iron and part of clay. Thou sawest till that a stone was cut out without hands, which smote the image upon his feet that were of iron and clay, and brake them to pieces. Then was the iron, the clay, the brass, the silver, and the gold, broken to pieces together, and became like the chaff of the summer threshingfloors; and the wind carried them away, that no place was found for them: and the stone that smote the image became a great mountain, and filled the whole earth. This is the dream; and we will tell the interpretation thereof before the king. Thou, O king, art a king of kings: for the God of heaven hath given thee a kingdom, power, and strength, and glory. And wheresoever the children of men dwell, the beasts of the field and the fowls of the heaven hath he given into thine hand, and hath made thee ruler over them all. Thou art this head of gold. And after thee shall arise another kingdom inferior to thee, and another third kingdom of brass, which shall bear rule over all the earth. And the fourth kingdom shall be strong as iron: forasmuch as iron breaketh in pieces and subdueth all things: and as iron that breaketh all these, shall it break in pieces and bruise. And whereas thou sawest the feet and toes, part of potters' clay, and part of iron, the kingdom shall be divided; but there shall be in it of the strength of the iron, forasmuch as thou sawest the iron mixed with miry clay. And as the toes of the feet were part of iron, and part of clay so the kingdom shall be partly strong, and partly broken. And whereas thou sawest iron mixed with miry clay, they shall mingle themselves with the seed of men: but they shall not cleave one to another, even as iron is not mixed with clay. And in the days of these kings shall the God of heaven set up a kingdom, which shall never be destroyed: and the kingdom shall not be left to other people, but it shall break in pieces and consume all these kingdoms, and it shall stand forever. Forasmuch as thou sawest that the stone was cut out of the mountain without hands, and that it brake in pieces the iron, the brass, the clay, the silver and the gold; the great God hath made known to the king what shall come to pass hereafter: and the dream is certain, and the interpretation is sure.

The first thing to note here is that Daniel says that this vision is a vision of the events of "the last days," therefore, this is not a vision of the events that would take place right after the death of Nebuchadnezzar. Yet, as one looks at this vision, it is uncanny how similar it is in describing the events soon after Nebuchadnezzar's life. I believe the reason this is so, is because the events that lead up to the tribulation period will closely track with the historic events that occurred from the Babylonian Conquest until Alexander the Great. Let's analyze this passage to identify the similarities.

Daniel says that Nebuchadnezzar, the king of Babylon, represents the golden head of the statue and the first kingdom. This kingdom is a kingdom over other *kingdoms*, a *world* superpower. I believe the gold represents a kingdom that is unmatched in its prosperity.

Daniel then mentions that the second kingdom is a kingdom of silver, and comes after Nebuchadnezzar. The silver indicates it is a kingdom of great wealth but not as wealthy as the first kingdom. Since this part of the statue represents the arms and chest, it is a divided kingdom like the arms are divided from one another; the divided kingdom of the Medes and the Persians.

The third kingdom of bronze that came after the Medes and the Persians (the kingdom of the belly and the thighs) represents a kingdom that is unified when it begins but then is divided in the same way that the belly is one part of the body and the thighs represents two parts. The "bronze" represents a kingdom that is militarily strong, but not necessarily economically strong, since bronze was used for weapons in the Bible but was not as valuable as silver or gold. It is apparent that Alexander the Great and the Greek Empire represented the kingdom of bronze. Alexander had a very strong military and he was a very strong unifying presence for his new kingdom. However, after his death, the kingdom became divided and was ruled by his three generals.

The fourth kingdom (the kingdom of the iron legs that became the iron and clay feet and toes) is a kingdom that is much more militarily strong than the bronze kingdom in the same way that iron is much stronger than bronze. Yet, it is as brittle as iron since it does break and the broken pieces are joined together with clay but the iron/clay feet represent a weak union. This kingdom represents the Roman Empire that came after the Greek Empire known for its military strength. The Roman Empire was also divided (the two iron legs represents a kingdom that had two parts) in the sense that it had two capitals: Rome and Constantinople (modern day Istanbul and Turkey). The Roman Empire represented a kingdom with two very diverse cultures: the European culture and the Middle Eastern culture.

If the events that occur before and during the tribulation parallel the description above, then we would expect the first world superpower of this era to be an economic powerhouse associated with Babylon. The second world power of this era would be very economically powerful, yet not as strong as the first and would be associated with the Medes and the Persians. The third world power would be militarily strong and rule the world, yet not as economically strong as the first two kingdoms and it would be associated with Greece. The fourth kingdom will be exceedingly strong militarily, yet be broken in pieces and form an unsteady alliance of countries and be associated with the two capitals of the Roman Empire: Rome and Constantinople.

We will use this information as a foundation to understand Daniel's vision of the four beasts.

Daniel's Vision of the Four Beasts

Later in his book, Daniel tells of a vision he has that describes four beasts.

Many theologians believe these beasts are kingdoms that arise in the last days that are analogous to the four empires described in Nebuchadnezzar's dream (Daniel 7:1–8):

> In the first year of Belshazzar king of Babylon, Daniel had a dream and visions of his head upon his bed: then he wrote the dream, and told the sum of the matters. Daniel spake and said, I saw in my vision by night, and, behold, the four winds of the heaven strove upon the great sea. And four great beasts came up from the sea, diverse one from another. The first was like a lion, and had eagle's wings: I beheld till the wings thereof were plucked, and it was lifted up from the earth, and made stand upon the feet as a man, and a man's heart was given to it. And behold another beast, a second, like a bear, and it raised up itself on one side, and it had three ribs in the mouth of it between the teeth of it: and they said thus unto it, Arise, devour much flesh. After this I beheld, and lo another, like a leopard, which had upon the back of it four wings of a fowl; the beast also four heads;

and dominion was given to it. After this I saw in the night visions, and behold a fourth beast, dreadful and terrible, and strong exceedingly, and it had great iron teeth: it devoured and brake in pieces, and stamped the residue with the feet of it: and it was diverse from all the beasts that were before it; and it had ten horns. I considered the horns, and, behold, there came up among them another little horn, before whom there were three of the first horns plucked up by the roots: and, behold, in this horn were eyes like the eyes of man, and a mouth speaking great things.

There are a few things to keep in mind while analyzing these beasts. First, all these beasts represent a partnership between multiple nations. Theologians have taken this approach with all the beasts except the first beast, and I will demonstrate in what manner it is a symbol of two separate nations.

Secondly, these beasts also represent the nations mentioned in Nebuchadnezzar's dream of the statue. For instance, the lion with the eagle's wings must be associated with the golden head of Nebuchadnezzar's statue; the bear with the three ribs in its mouth must be associated with the silver chest and arms of Nebuchadnezzar's statue, etc.

Thirdly, I believe the animals used to describe individual beasts depict the relative strength of the beasts. The lion is stronger than the bear; the bear is stronger than the leopard; the fourth beast is described as being "terrible" so I believe it is stronger than them all.

Finally, I believe these animals can be easily identified with their respective countries in the same way that the eagle is identified with the United States.

The First Beast: The Lion with Eagle's Wings

The first beast (the lion with eagle's wings) is probably the most enigmatic of all the beasts described. Most conservative theologians believe that the lion with eagle's wings represented Babylon (modern day Iraq), by comparing Babylon with the head of gold mentioned in Nebuchadnezzar's dream. Daniel stated that Nebuchadnezzar's kingdom, Babylon, represented the head of gold. Archaeologists have found several statues in ancient Babylon during the period of Nebuchadnezzar's reign of lions with eagle's wings, so it would appear this would be a relatively sound interpretation. I think there is something of significance missing. All of the other beasts are symbolic of many nations: the bear with the three ribs in its mouth is representative of four nations, the leopard with four heads is representative of (at least) four nations and the beast with ten horns is representative of (at least) ten nations. Is it possible that the lion with eagle's wings refers to multiple nations?

If you think of the first beast as two animals, a lion and an eagle, it becomes easier to visualize the interpretation of Daniel's vision regarding the first beast.

Consider three prophecies in the scriptures that involve eagles: 1) the riddle of the two eagles, 2) two eagle wings that transport the Jews to a safe refuge during the tribulation period, and 3) the description of Nebuchadnezzar being like an eagle during his seven-year period of insanity.

The Riddle of the Two Eagles

The riddle of the two eagles is described in Ezekiel 17:2–8:

> Son of man, put forth a riddle, and speak a parable unto the house of Israel; And say, thus saith the Lord God; a great eagle with great wings, longwinged, full of feathers, which had diverse colours, came unto Lebanon, and took the highest branch of the cedar: He cropped off the top of his young twigs, and carried it into a land of traffick; he set it in a city of merchants. He took also of the seed of the land, and planted it in a fruitful field; he placed it by great waters, and set it as a willow tree. And it grew, and became a spreading vine of low stature, whose branches turned toward him, and the roots thereof were under him: so it became a vine, and brought forth branches and shot forth sprigs. There was also another great eagle with great wings and many feathers: and, behold, this vine did bend her roots toward him, and shot forth her branches toward him, that he might water it by the furrows of her plantation. It was planted in a good soil by great waters, that it might bring forth branches, and that it might bear fruit, that it might be a goodly vine.

I believe this passage describes two nations that are very similar in their relationship to Israel. The first eagle is "a great eagle with great wings," so it is a powerful nation. It is "full of feathers," so it has many people. It is "longwinged," so it is located far away from Israel. It has "diverse colours," so it is nation of people of different colored skins (black, yellow, white, red, etc.). The eagle comes to Lebanon and takes a sprig from the highest branch of the cedar; the cedar of Lebanon is used in many places in the Old Testament to represent the people of Israel (Lebanon was actually part of the nation of Israel in the Old Testament). Therefore, the first eagle carries a small group from the nation of Israel and transplants them in the far removed country of the first eagle. They are transplanted in a "land of traffick" (a nation with a strong economy), and are set in a "city of merchants" (a city that is associated with trade).

If you pull all these descriptions together of the first eagle, it appears this parable is describing the United States and its relationship to Israel prior to the establishment of Israel as a nation in 1948. The United States, like the first eagle, is a large nation far removed from Israel that is an economic power with a "melting pot" of different colored peoples. Prior to and after 1948, many Jews settled in the United States and, more specifically, New York City, New York, which can be described as one of the world's largest centers of trade. The phrase "he took also the seed of the land, and planted in a fruitful field" refers to the United States involvement in the establishment of the Jewish people as a nation in Israel in 1948. The phrase "it became a vine of low stature" indicates that Israel, at least while the United States is still powerful, is a nation of lowly stature.

Then along comes the second eagle. It is a "great eagle with great feathers"; it is a powerful nation. Israel relies on this nation in the same way that Israel relies on the United States now. Israel becomes a goodly vine, a very prosperous nation during this period because of the trade it has with the second eagle. This second eagle represents the nation of the Antichrist (the "little horn") and also, as I described in chapter 1 of this book, the Kurds of northern Iraq.

I believe the lion with eagle's wings describes two nations, the United States and the Kurds of northern Iraq.

The Two Eagle's Wings

As I mentioned in chapter 1 of this book, I proposed that the "conspicuous horn" on the goat that is broken represents the end of the United States' position as the world's lone super-power sometime in the future. Also remember from chapter 1 of this book that the "conspicuous horn" is referred to as the first king. I propose that this "first king" refers to the first beast, the lion with the eagle's wings. Therefore, the eagle's wings are cut off of the lion; this is a picture of when the United States is no longer the world's lone superpower. These two eagle's wings occur in another instance in the scriptures (Revelation 12:14): "And to the woman were given two wings of a great eagle, that she might fly into the wilderness, into her place, where she is nourished for a time, and times, and half a time, from the face of the serpent."

I believe this scripture is referring to the time three and a half years into the tribulation when the United States (represented by the two eagle's wings) will return to Israel and transport the nation to a safe haven at a time when the United States is no longer the world's lone superpower.

Nebuchadnezzar Appears as an Eagle

Daniel the prophet records the events that lead to Nebuchadnezzar's seven-year period of insanity. Nebuchadnezzar demonstrates a lack of humility before God for his kingdom, so God punishes Nebuchadnezzar. Nebuchadnezzar apparently has the mind of an animal for seven years and ironically has the following symptoms (Daniel 4:32–33): "And they shall drive thee from men, and thy dwelling shall be with the beasts of the field: they shall make thee to eat grass as oxen, and seven times shall pass over thee, until thou know that the most High ruleth in the kingdom of men, and giveth it to whomsoever he will. The same hour was the thing fulfilled upon Nebuchadnezzar: and he was driven from men, and did eat grass as oxen, and his body was wet with the dew of heaven, till his hairs were grown like eagles' feathers, and his nails like birds' claws."

This passage is amazingly similar to the description of the lion with eagle's wings in that the lion is clipped of its wings and then rises to act like a man. Nebuchadnezzar acts like an animal, has some features of an eagle, for a period of seven years, and then regains his reason so that he can act like a man again. I believe the account of Nebuchadnezzar's insanity has a prophetic element to it. Nebuchadnezzar's illness is a picture of how the prophecy of the lion with eagle's wings would be fulfilled. I believe that the United States fulfills its role as the first eagle and then is broken as a world leader. Then, for a period of seven years, like Nebuchadnezzar, neither the United States nor the Kurds of Iraq are powerful nations. Three and half years into the tribulation, the Antichrist and the Kurds rise as the world superpower, seven years after the United States is devastated.

What the Bible Doesn't Say

The Bible doesn't always reveal everything God knows, and in the case of the first beast, this also appears to be true. There seems to be something missing in this interpretation of the vision of the first beast. How are the United States and the Kurds of northern Iraq related to one another? Recent events in the "war on terror" in Iraq may shed some light on this. When the U.S. soldiers entered northern Iraq and liberated the Kurds from the Saddam's reign of terror, one group among the Kurds was particularly glad to see them: the Yezedi.

The Yezedi are one of the religious groups among the Kurd. They were glad to see the U.S. troops because their religious writings prophesy the coming of holy people with red faces and blue eyes that would free them (Lawrence F. Kaplan, "Devil's Advocates," *The New Republic*, November 5, 2006, http://www.tnr.com/article/politics/75765/devils-advocate). Another web article said that many of them believed that a blue-eyed man will come from the west to free them from oppression (Cache Seel, "The Lost Faith," *Egypt Today*, December 2005, reprinted by World Media Watch: http://www.buzzflash.com/mediawatch/05/12/wmw05148.html). Is it possible that the Antichrist comes from America and sets up his future kingdom through this obscure religion?

The Yezidi are also unique for several other reasons. The most outstanding feature of their religion is that they worship Satan, the devil. They believe that rather than being punished by God in the Garden of Eden, that the serpent, Satan, was actually being rewarded. They worship Satan, and refer to him as Malak Taus, a term that literally means Peacock Angel. The Yezidi have taken great offense when their Muslim country-men end their prayers by saying such things as "God protect us from the devil." What better place would there be for the future Antichrist to establish as home base than a sect of devil worshippers?

The Second Beast:
The Bear with the Three Ribs

The first beast, the lion with the eagle's wings, is a truly amaz-ing description since the eagle is also the national symbol of the United States. I believe all the animals that describe the four beasts are the national symbols for those countries. If one had to guess what nation the second beast resembled, the bear with the three ribs in its mouth, I have no doubt that since the bear is the national symbol of Russia that very few people would not make this comparison.

However, I believe there is more to the bear. Since the bear is described as being higher on one side, then a comparison between two sides is being made. Therefore the bear must represent at least two nations: I believe the bear is a symbol for Russia and Iran.

The side that has raised itself is Iran, since during this time Iran will have raised itself as a powerful nation because it has control of the world's oil supply. I believe the three ribs in the bear's mouth, a symbol of three nations that have been stripped of their resources, are the three nations that Iran defeats as the ram described in Daniel chapter 8.

I have discussed previously in chapter 1 of this book, these nations that represent the three ribs are Turkey, Iraq, and Saudi Arabia. Let's look again at Daniel's description of the second beast (Daniel 8:5): "And suddenly another beast, a second, like a bear. It was raised up on one side, and had three ribs in its mouth between its teeth. And they said thus to it: 'Arise, devour much flesh!'" If you recall I also proposed that the second beast is the second nation mentioned in Nebuchadnezzar's dream. The second nation was the kingdom of silver that was described as the arms and chest of the statue. If we add all these prophetic imagery together we will end up with the following description of the second beast:

Since the second beast is a kingdom of silver I believe the second beast is a strong economic power, not as strong as the United States (the first beast, the kingdom of gold) but still an economic power. The two arms of the statue that represents the second beast indicate that it is a divided kingdom; the kingdom is made of two strong factions which are vying for control. The description of the bear raised up on one side indicates that one of the factions is very much stronger than the other, but the other faction, although weaker, still retains some amount of control over the kingdom. What is also very interesting about this five-nation consortium, is that the impoverished nations of the ribs also have some say in the actions of the bear since it does command the bear to go eat more flesh. Amazingly, the bear is not satisfied with the combined wealth of Turkey, Iraq, and Saudi Arabia!

Ezekiel's Vision of Gog

> And the word of the LORD came unto me, saying, Son
> of man, set thy face against Gog, the land of Magog,
> the chief prince of Meshech and Tubal, and proph-
> esy against him, And say, Thus saith the Lord GOD;
> Behold I am against thee, O Gog, the chief prince of
> Meshech and Tubal: And I will turn thee back, and put
> hooks into thy jaws, and I will bring thee forth, and all
> thine army, horses and horsemen, all of them clothed
> with all sorts of armour, even a great company with
> bucklers and shields, all of them handling swords:
> Persia, Ethiopia, and Libya with them; all of them with
> shield and helmet.
>
> EZEKIEL 38:1–5

While I am not the first, I believe that this passage describes
the invasion of Israel in the end times by a nation called Gog,
and Gog represents the modern-day nation of Russia. Many
scholars believe that Meschech and Tubal are ancient names
for the modern-day cities of Moscow and Tobolsk, Russia.

> Therefore, thou son of man, prophesy against Gog, and
> say, Thus saith the Lord GOD; Behold, I am against
> thee, O Gog, the chief prince of Meshech and Tubal:
> And I will turn thee back, and leave but the sixth part
> of thee, and will cause thee to come up from the north
> parts, and will bring thee upon the mountains of Israel:
> And I will smite thy bow out of thy left hand, and will
> cause thine arrows to fall out of thy right hand.

Thou shalt fall upon the mountains of Israel, thou, and all thy bands, and the people that is with thee: I will give thee unto the ravenous birds of every sort, and to the beasts of the field to be devoured. Thou shalt fall upon the open field: for I have spoken it, saith the Lord GOD. And I will send a fire on Magog, and among them that dwell carelessly in the isles: and they shall know that I am the LORD. So will I make my holy name known in the midst of my people Israel; and I will not let them pollute my holy name any more: and the heathen shall know that I am the

LORD, the Holy One in Israel.

EZEKIEL 39:1–7

This passage describes how God will protect Israel and how devastating the destruction that Russia will encounter will be. Russia's weapons will be knocked out of her hands and only one-sixth of Russia's forces will survive this encounter. The "isles" in this passage indicate that Europe is involved in this campaign and that God will also punish them for this offensive.

Behold, it is come, and it is done, saith the Lord GOD; this is the day whereof I have spoken. And they that dwell in the cities of Israel shall go forth, and shall set on fire and burn the weapons, both the shields and the bucklers, the bows and the arrows, and the handstaves, and the spears, and they shall burn them with fire seven years: So that they shall take no wood out of the field, neither cut down any out of the forests;

for they shall burn the weapons with fire: and they shall spoil those that spoiled them, and rob those that robbed them, saith the Lord GOD. And it shall come to pass in that day, that I will give unto Gog a place there of graves in Israel, the valley of the passengers on the east of the sea: and it shall stop the noses of the passengers: and there shall they bury Gog and all his multitude: and they shall call it The valley of Hamon-gog. And seven months shall the house of Israel be burying of them, that they may cleanse the land. Yea, all the people of the land shall bury them; and it shall be to them a renown the day that I shall be glorified, saith the Lord GOD. And they shall sever out men of continual employment, passing through the land to bury with the passengers those that remain upon the face of the earth, to cleanse it: after the end of seven months shall they search. And the passengers that pass through the land, when any seeth a man's bone, then shall he set up a sign by it, till the buriers have buried it in the valley of Hamon-gog. And also the name of the city shall be Hamonah. Thus shall they cleanse the land. And, thou son of man, thus saith the Lord GOD; Speak unto every feathered fowl, and to every beast of the field, Assemble yourselves, and come; gather your-selves on every side to my sacrifice that I do sacrifice for you, even a great sacrifice upon the mountains of Israel, that ye may eat flesh, and drink blood. Ye shall eat the flesh of the mighty, and drink the blood of the princes of the earth, of rams, of lambs, and of goats, of bullocks, all of them fatlings of Bashan. And ye shall eat fat till ye be full, and drink blood till ye be drunken, of my sacrifice which I have sacrificed for you. Thus ye shall be filled at my table with horses and chariots, with mighty men, and with all men of war, saith the Lord GOD. And I will set my glory among the heathen, and all the heathen shall see my judgment that I have executed, and my hand that I have laid upon them. So the house of Israel shall know that I am the LORD their God from that day and forward.

EZEKIEL 39:8–22

It is interesting to note that Israel will burn Russia's weapons for seven years and use them as an energy supply; I believe this seven-year period is the tribulation period. I believe this because the destruction of Russia, as Ezekiel writes about this further on in this chapter, marks the time when all the Jews return to Israel. The destruction of these armies will be an incredible event since it will take Israel seven months to bury all the bodies.

And the heathen shall know that the house of Israel went into captivity for their iniquity: because they trespassed against me, therefore hid I my face from them and gave them into the hand of their enemies: so fell they all by the sword. According to their uncleanness and according to their transgressions have I done unto them, and hid my face from them. Therefore thus saith the Lord GOD; Now will I bring again the captivity of Jacob, and have mercy upon the whole house of Israel, and will be jealous for my holy name; After that they have borne their shame, and all their trespasses whereby they have trespassed against me, when they dwelt safely in their land, and none made them afraid. When I have brought them again from the people, and gathered them out of their enemies' lands, and am sanctified in them in the sight of many nations; Then shall they know that I am the LORD their God, which cause them to be led into captivity among the heathen: but I have gathered them unto their own land, and have left none of them any more there. Neither will I hide my face any more from them: for I have poured out my spirit upon the house of Israel, saith the Lord GOD.

Ezekiel 39:23–29

It is obvious from the above passage that the destruction of the Russian bear in Israel marks the time when Israel's people that are spread throughout the world will finally return to Israel.

The Third Beast: The Leopard with Four Heads and Four Bird's Wings

As I have done with the other two beasts (the lion with eagle's wings and the bear with the three ribs in his mouth), let's assemble a complete image of the third beast: the leopard with four heads and four bird's wings.

The first thing to take note of is that this beast is the weakest of all the four beasts. The leopard is not as strong as a lion

48

or a bear, and certainly weaker than the fourth beast that is "terrible" in appearance. The leopard is also weak when you consider it has bird's wings, unlike the first beast that had eagle's wings; the bird being a much weaker animal than an eagle.

I believe the leopard is also symbolic of the multinational organization, the United Nations, embodied by the ram in Daniel's vision of the ram and the goat. I believe the four bird wings of the leopard are representative of all the countries in the world, because the four wings represent the four directions (north, south, east, and west). This is also shown in the book of Daniel (Daniel 2:39): "And after thee shall arise another kingdom inferior to thee, and another third kingdom of brass, which shall bear rule over all the earth." The leopard, the kingdom of brass, has the unique attribute of "having rule over all the earth." The four heads of the leopard are also consistent with the four horns that arise from the ram after the "notable" horn is broken, the four nations that arise from their respective part of the world to rule the United Nations. The evidence that the leopard, and consequently the United Nations, are not powerful in and of themselves is that dominion is *given* to them (Daniel 7:6).

Remember that the leopard is also representative of the third kingdom mentioned in Nebuchadnezzar's vision of a statue, the kingdom of bronze that forms the waist and the legs of the statue. The bronze represents a military power that is inferior in strength to the iron kingdom that represents the fourth kingdom. The bronze that forms the waist and then the legs also represents the idea that the third kingdom will be unified in the beginning but later it will be separated into several parts. This is, again, consistent with the image of the ram having one horn and then having it broken and replaced by four horns that rise up later.

The Fourth Beast

Unlike the previous three beasts, the fourth beast is not compared to an animal; it is so dreadful in appearance that Daniel can only describe its features. It is dreadful, terrible, and exceedingly strong. It has great, iron teeth. The fourth beast represents the fourth kingdom of Daniel chapter 2: the kingdom of iron. The kingdom of iron forms the legs of the great statue of Daniel chapter 2, and then the feet and toes are made of iron and clay. It shall begin its reign as strong as iron, destroying the nations of the world with a cruelty such as humankind has never seen. However, it will be converted into a nation that is strong in some aspects and weak in others. It will be strong in its cruelty in dealing with the world.

Exactly *how* it will be weak is a bit of enigma (consider Daniel 2:43): "And whereas thou sawest iron mixed with miry clay, they shall mingle themselves with the seed of men: but they shall not cleave one to another, even as iron is not mixed with clay."

Let's first look at the word "mingle" in the text. Often this word is used in describing the command that God made to the Israelites to not "mingle" with the Canaanites, i.e., don't intermarry with them. Now, consider the word "cleave." The word "cleave" is most notably used in the Old Testament when it says that Adam "cleaved" to his wife Eve. My belief is that the kingdom of iron is broken because the backbone of its society is broken (the wife/husband relationship). I believe that this verse describes a society where the women are the "iron," and while they are willing to procreate with men, that may very well be the only involvement that they have with the other sex. I believe the men in this kingdom represent the clay and are subservient to the women. The kingdom of the iron and clay toes may very well be a true matriarchal society where the interaction of men and women will be limited to sexual intercourse, and the family unit may be nonexistent.

The kingdom of the iron will lose some of its power when it is broken into ten kings as represented by the ten toes made of iron/clay. This is also reflected by the fact that the fourth beast has ten horns in its head (Daniel 7:23). After the ten kingdoms arise, a new kingdom shall arise and conquer three of the ten kingdoms. I believe *this* kingdom is the kingdom that comes up "last" (see Daniel 8:3), the kingdom that is one of the kingdoms of the "ram" mentioned in Daniel chapter 8, the kingdom of the Medes, the Kurds of Iraq. It is in the kingdom of the Kurds that the Antichrist will arise as king and begin his reign of terror.

3

Roadmap to the End Times

Daniel Chapter 11:
The Roadmap of the End Times

I believe that there is one ongoing issue in relation to Daniel chapter 11 that contributes to its murky interpretation more than any other: the *incorrect* understanding of Old Testament history. Conservative theologians hold that verses 1 through 3 describe Alexander the Great conquering the Persian Empire. Consider Daniel 11:2–3, "And now will I show thee the truth. Behold, there shall stand up yet three kings in Persia: and the fourth shall be richer than they all: and by his strength through his riches he shall stir up all against the realm of Greece. And a mighty king shall stand up, that shall rule with great dominion, and do according to his will."

It has been widely taught that these four kings are of the Persian Empire that Alexander the Great conquered in about 300 BC. The fourth king is believed to be the Persian king Xerxes and the "mighty king" in verse 3 is believed to refer to Alexander the Great. The events of verses 4 through 20 presumably describe historical events immediately after the death of Alexander, and then it becomes apparent that verse 21 describes the coming of the Antichrist, as it transitions abruptly to the end times.

This interpretation that the first part of Daniel chapter 11 is a description of events during the time of Alexander the Great, I believe, is in disagreement with the text. Daniel Chapter 11 is a prophecy that is spoken to Daniel from an angel that actually begins to speak to him in Daniel chapter 10. This angel specifically states that the "truth" he is about to tell him describes end-time events (Daniel 10:14): "Now I am come to make thee understand what shall befall thy people in the latter days: for yet the vision is for many days." The angel begins his description of the vision in the next chapter: Daniel 11. Therefore, if Daniel chapter 11 is a description of end time events, let's look at it in that light when we analyze it.

Let's start our analysis with Daniel 11:2: "And now will I [the angel] show thee [Daniel] the truth. Behold, there shall stand up yet three kings in Persia; and the fourth shall be far richer than they all: and by his strength through his riches he shall stir up all against the realm of Greece." Rather than a succession of Persian kings, suppose these three kings are the kings of the nations captured by the ram as described in Daniel chapter 8 (Daniel 8:4a): "I saw the ram pushing westward, and northward and southward: so that no beasts might stand before him..." Remember that in chapter 1 of this book, I identified these three nations as Iraq, Turkey, and Saudi Arabia. What I am suggesting is that these three new kings are Iranian leaders, selected to represent the nations of Iraq, Turkey, and Saudi Arabia that have been captured by or even possibly the defeated rulers of these countries themselves. These nations are absorbed into Iran. Therefore, I believe this verse is describing a situation in which there will be four kings ruling Iran simultaneously. The real power is with the fourth king however; he is the leader of Iran. The fourth king will plunder the other three nations such that he controls all of the nations' wealth; this is why he will be "richer than them all." This also explains the image of the second beast of Daniel's vision in Daniel chapter 7: the bear with the three ribs in its mouth. These three ribs are a description of the nations of Iraq, Turkey, and Saudi Arabia. The wealth of these nations will be picked clean by Iran and Russia (Iran and Russia represent the bear) such that these "ribs" have no meat left on them. How will the fourth king (the leader of Iran) use these riches to "stir up all against the realm of Greece"? Much like Iran already does. They will use oil as a diplomatic weapon. The "realm of Greece" (the United Nations) will try to punish Iran for its invasion of Turkey, Iraq, and Saudi Arabia using economic sanctions, but Iran will thwart these efforts by offering cheap oil to those nations willing to stand with Iran.

Now, let's look at the next verse (Daniel 11:3): "And a mighty king shall stand up, that shall rule with great dominion, and do according to his will." What do we know about this king? This king is a Kurd. We know this because of Daniel 8:3b, "a ram which had two horns: and the two horns were high: but one was higher than the other, and the higher came up last." We know the two horns represent people of Iran and the Kurds but we also know that the Iranians are in power first, so the Iranians represent the first horn. Therefore, this king (the last king of Iran and the second horn of the ram) will be a Kurd. When this verse says, "he shall rule with great dominion," honestly, I doubt we can even comprehend how much control this ruler will wield over the world since Iran has control over the majority of the world's oil supply. This verse implies there will be absolutely no resistance from the world and Iran will be able to do whatever it wishes. However, we will see in the next verse that this is a short-lived situation.

"And when he shall stand up, his kingdom shall be broken, and shall be divided toward the four winds of heaven: and not to his posterity, nor according to his dominion which he ruled: for his kingdom will be plucked up, even for others besides those" (Daniel 11:4).

I believe this verse is a reference to the defeat the ram will experience at the hands of the goat that Daniel talks about in Daniel chapter 8. Not long after the Kurdish king of Iran arises to power, the United States (with the endorsement of the United Nations) will then absolutely crush Iran militarily. How will Iran be divided toward the four winds of heaven? This isn't too hard to visualize actually: Iraq to the west, Iran to the east, Turkey to the north, and Saudi Arabia to the south. However, there may be another possibility. When the United States (the horn of the goat) is broken and the United Nations is broken into four parts, is it possible that the four-nation union under Iran is divided among the four parts of the former United Nations? If so, then this would ensure there would be parity in oil resources for each of these four United Nations organizations.

The remaining portion of this verse addresses the question: What do you do with Iran? Something must be done to prevent them from trying this again. I believe the world will be so angry at Iran that they will take extremely drastic measures to make Iran powerless. They will literally disperse the nation of Iran across the whole earth. As this verse says, Iran is broken, but "not to his [the king's] posterity" (not to his people); Iranians will no longer live in Iran. His kingdom will be "plucked up" (exiled). This will be the fulfillment of Jeremiah's prophecy for Elam (Jeremiah 49:35–39):

> Thus saith the Lord of hosts: Behold, I will break the bow of Elam (Iran), the chief of their might. And upon Elam will I bring the four winds from the four quarters of heaven, and will scatter them toward all those winds, and there shall be no nation whither the outcasts of Elam shall not come. For I will cause Elam to be dismayed before their enemies, and before them that seek their life: and I will bring evil upon them, even my fierce anger, saith the Lord, and I will send the sword after them, till I have consumed them: And I will set my throne in Elam, and will destroy from thence the king and the princes, saith the Lord. But it shall come to pass in the latter days, that I will bring again the captivity of Elam, saith the Lord.

Note the similarity of Jeremiah's prophecy with Daniel's writings. Look how Jeremiah describes that Elam will be scattered among "the four winds," just as the kingdom of the "mighty king" of Daniel 11:4 "shall be divided toward the four winds of heaven." The goat was "moved with anger against" the ram in Daniel 8:7; the Lord brings His fierce anger upon Elam in Jeremiah 49:37. Also note that Elam will be shown no mercy: they are "consumed" and the king and princes are "destroyed." Therefore, the "mighty king," the last king of Iran (Daniel 11:4), and his princes (the three kings of Turkey, Iraq, and Saudi Arabia?) apparently die during this battle. There is good news for Elam though: the Lord promises to return the "captivity of Elam" to their home in "the latter days."

The implications of Daniel 11:4 are staggering.

The tremendously powerful ruler of Iran that will cause the world to bend to his desires will cause his nation to be crushed by the United States. His nation will be punished for its actions by the world with a severity we have never seen before in modern times. The world's sole superpower, the United States, will become "broken" and the result will be dramatic for the United Nations: the United Nations will be split into four separate entities, each led by a different world superpower, yet the United States will not be among them.

The Rise of the African Nation

> And the king of the south shall be strong, and one of his princes; and he shall be strong above him, and have dominion; his dominion shall be a great dominion.
>
> DANIEL 11:5

The king of the south arises to power in Daniel 11:5, as well as one of princes. Who is the "king of the south"? When the U.N. is organized into four regions, these regions will be divided according to direction, and the southern region will be Africa. The continent of Africa will rise in power like no time in history. The king of the south (presumably the king of Egypt, based on Daniel 11:8) and another ruler of Africa, maybe in Egypt or maybe elsewhere in Africa, rise to power according to Daniel 11:5, the king of Egypt being more powerful than the other ruler.

> And in the end of years they shall join themselves together; for the king's daughter of the south shall come to the king of the north to make an agreement: but she shall not retain the power of the arm; neither shall he stand, nor his arm: but she shall be given up, and they that brought her, and he that begot her, and he that strengthened her in these times.
>
> DANIEL 11:6

Verse 6 marks the last years prior to the seven-year tribulation period by starting with the phrase, "And in the end of years." The daughter of the king of Egypt will make a peace agreement with the king of the north. Who is the king of the north? As we will see below in Daniel 11:15, it is obvious that the king of the north represents Russia, and Russia is the superpower that rules the northern region of the United Nations. As Daniel 11:6 states, the king of Egypt, his subordinate ruler, and his daughter are somehow captured during this effort to sign a peace treaty with Russia.

> But out of a branch of her roots shall one stand up in his estate, which shall come with an army, and shall enter into the fortress of the king of the north, and shall deal against them, and shall prevail: And shall also carry captives into Egypt their gods, with their

princes, and with their precious vessels of silver and of gold; and he shall continue more years than the king of the north. So the king of the south shall come into his kingdom, and shall return into his own land.

DANIEL 11:7–9

A ruler that is related to the daughter of the king of Egypt (Daniel 11:7) rises to power, organizes an army against Russia, and prevails. He brings to Egypt their gods (a reference to which we are still unclear), princes, and silver/gold.

But his sons shall be stirred up, and shall assemble a multitude of great forces: and one shall certainly come, and overflow, and pass through: then shall he return, and be stirred up, even to his fortress. And the king of the south shall be moved with anger, and shall come forth and fight with him, even with the king of the north: and he shall set forth a great multitude; but the multitude shall be given into his hand. And when he hath taken away the multitude, his heart shall be lifted up; and he shall cast down many ten thousands: but he shall not be strengthened by it.

DANIEL 11:10–12

The sons of the king of Russia (Daniel 11:10–12) seek revenge on Egypt by organizing a great army and attack Egypt. When Russia "passes through" and "returns," they are going through Israel. Egypt responds by attacking with a great army. Even though Egypt destroys "tens of thousands" of the Russians, they are not "strengthened by the victory."

"For the king of the north shall return, and shall set forth a multitude greater than the former, and shall certainly come after certain years with a great army and with much riches. And in those times there shall many stand up against the king of the south: also the robbers of thy people shall exalt themselves to establish the vision; but they shall fall" (Daniel 11:13–14).

The king of Russia returns (Daniel 11:13) with a larger force than his sons to once again attack Egypt and Daniel 11:14b suggests many countries will join in the attack: "shall many stand up against the king of the south." Several details from Daniel 11:13–14 show that this campaign against Egypt by Russia includes the invasion of Israel by Russia described in Ezekiel chapter 38: the infamous invasion of Israel by Gog of Magog. Since many countries are involved, this is certainly consistent with Ezekiel chapter 38 since it describes Persia, Ethiopia, Libya, and the bands of Gomer (the European nations) rising with Magog (Russia) against Israel. The phrase in Daniel 11:14, "the robbers of thy people [Israel]," is consistent with the following verses from Ezekiel 38:11–13:

And thou shalt say, I will go up to the land of unwalled villages; I will go to them that are at rest, that dwell safely, all of them dwelling without walls, and having neither bars nor gates. To take a spoil, and to take a prey; to turn thine hand upon the desolate places that are now inhabited, and upon the people that are gathered out of the nations, which have gotten cattle and goods, that dwell in the midst of the land. Sheba (Yemen) and Dedan (Saudi Arabia), and the merchants of Tarshish (Spain?), with all the young lions thereof, shall say unto thee, Art thou come to take a spoil? Hast thou gathered thy company to take a prey? To carry away silver and gold, to take away cattle and goods, to take a great spoil?

Daniel 11:14b ominously states that the effort to rob Israel will come to a disastrous conclusion: "but they shall fall." Ezekiel 38:22–23 describes it this way: "And I will plead against him [Russia] with pestilence and with blood; and I will rain upon him, and upon his bands, and upon the many people that are with him, an overflowing rain, and great hailstones, fire and brimstone. Thus will I magnify myself, and sanctify myself; and I will be known in the eyes of many nations, and they shall know that I am Lord."

"So the king of the north shall come, and cast up a mount, and take the most fenced cities: and the arms of the south shall not withstand, neither his chosen people, neither shall there be any strength to withstand. But he that cometh against him shall do according to his own will, and none shall stand before him: and he shall stand in the glorious land, which by his hand shall be consumed" (Daniel 11:15–16).

Daniel 11:15–16 tells that Russia will overcome Egypt ("the arms of the south") and will wreak havoc on the "glorious land" (Israel) and the "chosen people" (the people of Israel).

"He shall also set his face to enter with the strength of his whole kingdom, and upright ones with him; thus shall he do: and he shall give him the daughter of women, corrupting her: but she shall not stand on his side, neither be for him" (Daniel 11:17).

Here in Daniel 11:17, after it invades Israel, then Russia invades Egypt with all of its forces and brings with it captives from Israel ("upright ones"). One of the most enigmatic phrases in the study of prophecy is the description of the person who is the "daughter of women." Apparently the king of Egypt gives the daughter of women to the king of Russia. How she is corrupted is confusing: was she raped, or was she caused to worship idols, or both? How can she really be "corrupted" if she isn't a Jew? While this term "daughter of women" is not used in any other place in scripture, there *is* a description of a "daughter" of Egypt that sounds amazingly similar to this woman. This reference to a "daughter" of Egypt occurs in Jeremiah chapter 46:

"Go up into Gilead, and take balm, O virgin, the daughter of Egypt: in vain shalt thou use many medicines; for thou shalt not be cured. The nations have heard of thy shame, and thy cry hath filled the land: for the mighty man hath stumbled against the mighty, and they are fallen both together" (Jeremiah 46:11–12).

"O thou daughter dwelling in Egypt, furnish thyself to go into captivity: for Noph shall be waste and desolate without an inhabitant" (Jeremiah 46:19).

"The daughter of Egypt shall be confounded; she shall be delivered into the hand of the people of the north" (Jeremiah 46:24).

Looking at Jeremiah 46:11, why should the daughter of Egypt go to take balm from Gilead (which is in Israel)? Earlier in the book of Jeremiah, Jeremiah describes how the balm of Gilead, a medicine from the mountainous region in Israel, couldn't even cure the (spiritual) sickness of Israel because of their rebellion against God (Jeremiah 8:22): "Is there no balm in Gilead; is there no physician there? Why then is not the health of the daughter of my people recovered?" Therefore, Jeremiah 46:11 may be an indication that the "daughter of women" that comes from Egypt is originally from Israel. It is also interesting to note here in Jeremiah 46:11 that this daughter is a virgin, a woman not given in marriage yet, while the "daughter of women" in Daniel 11:17 has just been given in marriage to the king of Russia. It appears that this corruption that the "daughter of women" experiences is a rebellion against her God (since she is originally from Israel). Jeremiah 46:19 also points out that the "daughter of women" is a woman who was dwelling in Egypt and now will be in captivity. Note also that the word "confounded" in Jeremiah 46:24 can also be translated as "ashamed"; this could explain why the "daughter of women" will not stand by or be for her new husband, the king of Russia (since she is ashamed of him).

> After this shall he turn his face unto the isles, and shall take many: but a prince for his own behalf shall cause the reproach offered by him to cease; without his own reproach he shall cause it to turn upon him. Then he shall turn his face toward the fort of his own land: but he shall stumble and fall, and not be found.
>
> DANIEL 11:18–19

Russia will then invade the "isles" (Europe) and will take several countries (verse 18), and then the king of Russia returns home where he meets his end (verse 19). "Then shall stand up in his estate a raiser of taxes in the glory of the kingdom: but within few days he shall be destroyed, neither in anger, nor in battle" (Daniel 11:20).

Daniel 11:20 introduces the next king of Russia that is a "raiser of taxes" and reigns for only a few days. Isaiah 23:15 describes the rise of the city of Tyre as a strong economic power and it is associated with the short reign of a king also: "And it shall come to pass in that day, that Tyre shall be forgotten seventy years, according to the days of one king: after the end of seventy years shall Tyre sing as a harlot."

The word "days" in this verse literally means days, so this verse can be interpreted to mean that after seventy years (presumably the king's reign mentioned in this verse only lasts seventy days) Tyre would rise in power as a great merchant city that plays a pivotal role in the reign of the "Antichrist" in the tribulational period mentioned in the book of Revelation. I believe that the life of this king that is mentioned in Daniel 11:20 that has a reign of seventy days will mark the rise of the city of Tyre. The city of Tyre is important in the events of the tribulational period, because it is the wealth of Tyre that supplies the Antichrist with his political power during this time. Not surprisingly, the next king to replace the king with the reign of seventy days is the Antichrist as described in Daniel 11:21: "And in his estate shall stand up a vile person, to whom they shall not give the honor of the kingdom: but he shall come in peaceably, and obtain the kingdom by flatteries."

As I have mentioned in the discussion on Daniel chapter 8, the Antichrist arises from a small country (I believe he will rule the Kurds of Iraq) and this is described here in Daniel

11:23: "And after the league made with him he shall work deceitfully: for he shall come up, and shall become strong with a small people."

Now, remember that the purpose of this book, *Living in the Age of the Ram and the Goat*, is to describe events that happen prior to the tribulation. Since the appearance of the Antichrist marks the beginning of the seven-year tribulational period, I must stop the analysis of Daniel Chapter 11 at verse 23. However, since the Antichrist is an integral part of the first beast (the lion with eagle's wings), I have devoted the next chapter to discussing the Antichrist.

4

The Antichrist

He is the Man from Dan

Many people who dabble in the study of end-times prophecy and the Antichrist often pose the following question, "Do you think they (usually some prominent Hollywood or political personality) are the Antichrist?" If you know some basic information about the Antichrist, it is often very easy to exclude many of the people proposed to be the Antichrist.

First of all, many theologians believe that the Antichrist is a descendant of the tribe of Dan (one of the sons of Jacob mentioned in the book of Genesis). There are two prominent biblical references that provide support for this idea: Genesis 49:17 and Revelation chapter 7. Genesis 49:17 is the blessing (or cursing) that Dan receives from Jacob just before Jacob dies: "Dan shall be a serpent in the way, a horned snake in the path..."

Since Satan spoke through the serpent in the Garden of Eden when he tempted Eve, the serpent has been seen as his symbol. Therefore, comparing Dan and his descendants to a serpent is a special connection of Dan with Satan. Revelation chapter 7 also provides additional evidence that the tribe of Dan is the tribe of the Antichrist. This chapter lists the twelve tribes of Israel that will be "sealed" with God's seal on their foreheads. The tribe of Dan is not mentioned in that list. If the tribe of Dan is the tribe of the Antichrist, and is carrying out the plans of Satan in opposition to God, it would make perfect sense that Dan's people would not receive the seal of God. Therefore, we can see that the Antichrist has several characteristics based on this information: he is a descendant of Dan (and consequently must be of Middle East/Asian descent) and has a special relationship to Satan. Therefore, if the person you propose to be the Antichrist doesn't at least have some evidence of Middle Eastern ancestry in their DNA, they are not the Antichrist.

He is the King of Tyre and Babylon

There are two scriptures in the Old Testament that are particularly interesting in that they both form a very descriptive picture of Satan; these passages are Ezekiel chapter 28 and Isaiah chapter 14. What is also interesting about these passages is that Satan is given two different (apparently "earthly") titles. Satan is referred to as the King of Tyrus in Ezekiel chapter 28 and he is referred to as the King of Babylon in Isaiah chapter 14. So why is Satan given these titles? I believe it is connected to Satan's relationship to the Antichrist. The Antichrist will be the result of the ultimate act of demon-possession by the ultimate demon. Think of the Antichrist as Satan in the flesh. I believe that Satan will have "possessed" the mortal person who is the Antichrist, and the actions of the Antichrist will be indistinguishable from the actions of Satan. Therefore, I believe that if we examine these two scriptures recognizing this relationship between the Antichrist and Satan, we will be better equipped to interpret these passages completely.

Tyre was an ancient city that was located on the coast of modern Lebanon, which had made its fortune from trading with other countries in the Mediterranean Sea. Tyre was also particularly interesting because of its role in the construction of Solomon's Temple. Hiram, the king of Tyre during the reign of David, was contracted by Solomon to provide cedar and fir from Lebanon for the construction of the Temple. Hiram's men were also gifted in masonry, and so they also carved stones that were used in the Temple. Hiram also appears to have been an artisan in brass, so Solomon also used him and his people to provide any items made of brass that were used in the Temple.

I mentioned all of this about Hiram because the scriptures indicate that the Antichrist will arise on the scene at first as a successful merchant, the king of Tyre, and he will become rich much the same way that Hiram did. He will sell materials for the construction of the next Temple in Jerusalem.

Ezekiel 28:1-19

Now, let's consider Ezekiel chapter 28 since it talks about the king of Tyre:

> The word of the Lord came again unto me, saying, Son of man, say unto the prince of Tyrus, Thus saith

the Lord God; Because thine heart is lifted up, and thou hast said, I am a God, I sit in the seat of God, in the midst of the seas; yet thou art a man, and not God, though thou set thine heart as the heart of God: Behold, thou art wiser than Daniel; there is no secret that they can hide from thee: With thy wisdom and with thine understanding thou hast gotten thee riches, and hast gotten gold and silver into thy treasures: By thy great wisdom and by thy traffick hast thou increased thy riches, and thine heart is lifted up because of thy riches: Therefore thus saith the Lord God; Because thou hast set thine heart as the heart of God; Behold, therefore I will bring strangers upon thee, the terrible of the nations: and they shall draw their swords against the beauty of thy wisdom, and they shall defile thy brightness. They shall bring thee down to the pit, and thou shalt die the deaths of them that are slain in the midst of the seas. Wilt thou yet say before him that slayeth thee, I am God? But thou shalt be a man, and no God, in the hand of him that slayeth thee. Thou shalt die the deaths of the uncircumcised by the hand of strangers: for I have spoken it, saith the Lord God. Moreover the word of the Lord came unto me, saying, Son of man, take up a lamentation upon the king of Tyrus, and say unto him, Thus saith the Lord God; Thou sealest up the sum, full of wisdom, and perfect in beauty. Thou hast been in Eden the garden of God; every precious stone was thy covering, the sardius, topaz, and the diamond, the beryl, the onyx, and the jasper, the sapphire, the emerald and the carbuncle and gold: the workmanship of thy tabrets and of thy pipes was prepared in thee in the day that thou wast created. Thou art the anointed cherub that covereth; and I have set thee so: thou wast upon the holy mountain of God; thou hast walked up and down in the midst of the stones of fire. Thou wast perfect in thy ways from the day that thou wast created, till iniquity was found in thee. By the multitude of thy merchandise they have filled the midst of thee with violence, and thou hast sinned: therefore I will cast thee as profane out of the mountain of God: and I will destroy thee, O covering cherub, from the midst of the stones of fire. Thine heart was lifted up because of thy beauty, thou has corrupted thy wisdom by reason of thy brightness: I will cast thee to the ground, I will lay thee before kings, that they may behold thee. Thou hast defiled thy sanctuaries by the multitude of thine iniquities, by the iniquity of thy traffick; therefore will I bring forth a fire from the midst of thee, it shall devour thee, and I will bring thee to ashes upon the earth in the sight of all them that behold thee. All they that know thee among the people shall be astonished at thee: thou shalt be a terror, and never shalt thou be any more.

EZEKIEL 28:1–19

An overview of this chapter reveals the following structure:

Verses 1–11 describe the Antichrist as a man who claims to be the Christian God (verse 2), and a man who is very smart and uses his intelligence to become a very rich businessman.

It is his wealth that puffs him up with pride so that he aspires to be a god.

Verses 7–10 describe how the nations will revolt against him and ultimately destroy him.

Verse 10 provides an interesting clue that the Antichrist is a descendant of Israel: the Antichrist shall "die the death of the uncircumcised." The verse insinuates that the Antichrist will die a death that is a shameful one for someone who is circumcised or, more directly, is shameful to someone who is a descendant of Israel. If the Antichrist is a descendant of the tribe of Dan as I mentioned previously, this certainly would make sense.

Verses 12–15 then transitions into descriptions that can only be true of Satan.

Verse 13 describes how the King of Tyre had been in the Garden of Eden. Since we know from the book of Genesis that only God, Adam, Eve, and Satan have ever been there, then this certainly is a description of Satan.

Verse 14 certainly makes it more clear that this is Satan, since it refers to him as the anointed angel that resided in the very presence of God.

Verse 15 laments the downfall of Satan in that he was faithful to God in the beginning, but later sin is found in him.

Verses 16–19 then transitions into a description that seem to unite the persons of Satan and the Antichrist. These verses describe how Satan will be cast out of heaven to the earth and destroyed, which causes one to ask, "How can you destroy an angel? Aren't angels spiritual beings that do not have physical bodies?"

Verse 18 describes how Satan will be brought to "ashes."

Only a person with a physical body can be consumed by fire to produce ashes. Verse 19 also seems to describe a mortal person since it says, "All they that know thee among the people…" This verse seems to point to the possibility that there will be people who will personally know Satan; how is this possible unless he is living among them in a human body? The persons of Satan and the Antichrist are also tied together in these verses because Satan is described with characteristics that were used to describe the king of Tyre (the Antichrist) earlier in this chapter.

Verse 16 describes how Satan's "merchandise" has caused him to sin, and verse 18 states how his sanctuaries are defiled by the sin of his "traffick" (or commercial goods). Remember in verse 5 of this chapter that the king of Tyre is made rich by his "traffick." Therefore, I believe that the writer of this chapter, by repeating the use of this same word "traffick," is trying to send the message to us that the king of Tyre, the Antichrist, is Satan in a mortal body here on earth during the tribulational period.

What may occur to the reader is that Jesus came to the earth in a similar fashion in that He was God made flesh. This is not a coincidence; in fact it is the purpose of Satan to mimic Christ so that he may portray himself as the Messiah to all mankind.

Isaiah 14:4–19

Now, let's conduct an overview of Isaiah chapter 14, and note the similarities between it and Ezekiel chapter 28:

That thou shalt take up this proverb against the king of Babylon, and say, How hath the oppressor ceased! The Lord hath broken the staff of the wicked, and the scepter of the rulers. He who smote the people in wrath with a continual stroke, he that ruled the nations in anger, is persecuted, and none hindereth. The whole earth is at rest, and is quiet: they break forth into singing. Yea, the fir trees rejoice at thee, and the cedars of Lebanon, saying, Since thou art laid down, no feller is come up against us. Hell from beneath is moved for thee to meet thee at thy coming: it stirreth up the dead for thee, even all the chief ones of the earth; it hath raised up from their thrones all the kings of the nations. All they shall speak and say unto thee, Art thou also become weak as we? Art thou become like unto us? Thy pomp is brought down to the grave, and the noise of thy viols: the worm is spread under thee, and the worms cover thee. How art thou fallen from heaven, O Lucifer, son of the morning! How art thou cut down to the ground, which didst weaken the nations! For thou hast said in thine heart, I will ascend into heaven, I will exalt my throne above the stars of God: I will sit also upon the mount of the congregation, in the sides of the north: I will ascend above the heights of the clouds; I will be like the most High. Yet thou shalt be brought down to hell, to the sides of the pit. They that see thee shall narrowly look upon thee, and consider thee, saying, Is this the man that made the earth to tremble, that did shake kingdoms; That made the world as a wilderness, and destroyed the cities thereof; that opened not the house of his prisoners? All the kings of the nations, even all of them, lie in glory, every one in his own house. But thou art cast out of thy grave like an abominable branch, and as the raiment of those that are slain, thrust through with a sword, that go down to the stones of the pit; as a carcase trodden under feet.

Isaiah 14:4–19

Starting with verse four, we see the object of this text is the king of Babylon:

Verses 4–8 describes how the king of Babylon (the Antichrist) is brought down as well as his city (presumably the city of Babylon). These verses describe him as being particularly oppressive to all the nations or the earth.

Verse 8 describes how the citizens of Lebanon are relieved at his destruction. What is interesting in this statement is that Lebanon is the country where the city of Tyre is located. Is it possible that the king of Babylon is also the king of Tyre? I believe he is.

Verse 9–10 describes how hell has resurrected the kings of the earth that the king of Babylon has killed, so that they may deride him for being "weak" like they are. Ezekiel 28:17 also describes Satan's destruction such that he will fall "before kings, that they may behold thee." This comparison provides supporting information that the king of Babylon, Satan, and the king of Tyre are the same man.

Verse 12 also renames the king of Babylon by calling him

Lucifer (Satan's other name in the scriptures). Here, Lucifer is "cut down to the ground," while in Ezekiel 28:17, Satan is "cast" down to the ground.

Verses 13–14 describes how Lucifer will attempt to claim a throne in heaven and how he will be like God, just like Satan's description as God's angel in Ezekiel chapter 28. How can the king of Babylon, a mortal king, take on the characteristics of a spiritual being: Lucifer the angel? We are left with a similar conclusion here as in Ezekiel chapter 28, which is that the king of Babylon is a man that is possessed by Lucifer the evil angel.

Verse 19 is the final similarity between these two passages. This verse is a reference to the king of Babylon being a descendant of Israel, just as the king of Tyre is a descendant of Israel. Isaiah 14:19 calls the king of Babylon "an abominable branch"; the term "branch" is used in other portions of scripture to describe descendants of Israel. Joseph is called a branch in the book of Genesis and Jesus Christ is certainly known as The Branch. As a reminder, Ezekiel chapter 28 describes the death of king of Tyre as a death of the uncircumcised, thus suggesting the king of Tyre was a descendant of Israel because of this symbolic representation of circumcision.

Therefore, the king of Babylon and the king of Tyre are both descendants of Israel.

These two passages make it very clear that Satan will be "one" with the Antichrist. This information causes one to speculate how this relationship works between Satan and the Antichrist. I believe the New Testament does provide some enlightenment. It is recorded in Luke chapter 4 that Jesus

Christ is tempted by Satan in the wilderness. It is very interest-ing to note one of the things that Satan offers Jesus to induce Him to worship Satan (Luke 4:5–7): "And the devil [Satan], taking him [Jesus] up into an high mountain, showed unto him all the kingdoms of the world in a moment of time. And the devil said unto him, All this power will I give thee, and the glory of them: for that is delivered unto me; and to whomso-ever I will I give it. If thou therefore wilt worship me, all shall be thine."

I believe very few people actually understand the impli-cations of this passage of scripture. The first thing to under-stand about this situation is that Satan is not equal to God in his power. God is omnipotent (all-powerful), omniscient (all-knowing), and omnipresent (present everywhere at anytime). Satan does not have any of these powers; in fact, any power Satan owns has been given him since God created him (see Ezekiel 28:13): "...the workmanship of thy tabrets and of thy pipes was prepared in thee in the day that thou wast created." (My personal belief is that we give credit to Satan for more than he is capable of. I believe that our fight is primarily with the flesh in addition to struggles with his demons so it is not necessary for Satan to be omnipresent, while it may seem that he is. I believe that Satan has very specific targets of people highly revered by God such as Job, David, Jesus, etc.)

We see this clearly when Satan seeks to destroy Job (Job chapter 1) and God gives him the power to do so and also defines Satan's limitations (Job 1:12): "And the Lord said unto Satan, Behold, all that he [Job] hath is in thy power; only upon himself put not forth thine hand." We also see that in the encounter between Satan and Jesus that Satan's power to give Jesus all the kingdoms of the world has been "delivered" to him (given to him). This means *God* gave this to him.

Why would God do this? Some may say this was so that Satan could tempt Jesus; I believe it was something different. I believe this was a power given to Satan by God to accomplish God's plan for the Antichrist. I believe this offer that Satan makes Jesus is the same offer Satan will make to the Antichrist. Think about it. Since Jesus rejected his offer, Satan should still have the ability to offer the world to anyone he wishes. Also think about the terrible ramifications if Jesus did accept; it is clear to me that Satan wanted to use Jesus to accomplish all the awful acts that are attributed to the Antichrist in the book of Revelation. How blessed we are that Jesus turned him down! Therefore, if I am correct, then Satan has known for at least two thousand years that he will pick the Antichrist to rule the world. So, what does this passage in Luke have to say about the Antichrist? Satan said he would give the kingdoms of the world and all their glory (riches) to Jesus, if He would worship Satan. I believe that the Antichrist must be a worshipper of Satan to accept Satan's offer.

He is the Assyrian

The Antichrist is referred to as "the Assyrian" in the Old Testament twelve times while the term "Antichrist" is only used four times to describe him in the New Testament. If the Antichrist is indeed an Assyrian in the modern-day sense of the description, then this is a very specific clue as to his identity. The world's population of Assyrians is only 4.5 million people according to the Assyrian International News Agency Web site. This fact in and of itself drastically limits the potential suspects.

What is more interesting about this piece of information is that the Assyrian people, just like the Kurds (the people that I identified in chapter 1 as the kingdom that the Antichrist uses to rise to power), do not have a country that they can claim as their own. The land that the Assyrians claim as their territory and the land the Kurds claim but do not own are, in fact, the same territory. Is it possible that the Antichrist's nation, the little horn of Daniel chapter 8, will be comprised of Assyrians and Kurds? I believe this will be the case.

So what does the Old Testament have to say about the Assyrian? "O Assyrian, the rod of mine anger, and the staff in their hand is mine indignation" (Isaiah 10:5).

Isaiah chapter 10 describes how the Assyrian is used by God to punish Israel during the tribulation period because Israel has become a hypocritical nation that has robbed their own poor and widows for their possessions. After this period of punishment ends, the Lord will punish the Assyrian (Isaiah 10:24).

"Behold the land of the Chaldeans; this people was not, till the Assyrian founded it for them that dwell in the wilderness: they set up the towers thereof, they raised up the palaces thereof; and he brought it to ruin" (Isaiah 23:13). This verse provides evidence that the Assyrian is the Antichrist; the Assyrian, just like the Antichrist, establishes a people that have no land and have no kingdom.

"And this man shall be the peace, when the Assyrian shall come into our land: and when he shall tread in our palaces, then shall we raise against him seven shepherds, and eight principal men" (Micah 5:5).

Micah 5:1

Micah chapter 5 provides evidence that the Assyrian is from the tribe of Dan. Let's start the analysis from the beginning of the chapter (Micah 5:1): "Now gather thyself in troops, O daughter of troops: he hath laid siege against us: they shall smite the judge of Israel with a rod upon the cheek." I believe this verse is referring to two different tribes of Israel. If you look at Genesis 49:16–19, you can see the analogy: "Dan shall judge his people, as one of the tribes of Israel. Dan shall be a serpent by the way, an adder in the path, that biteth the horse heels, so that his rider shall fall backward. I have waited for thy salvation, O Lord. Gad, a troop shall overcome him [Dan]: but he shall overcome at the last." As I have already pointed out that Dan is the tribe of the Antichrist; these verses point out that Gad is the tribe that will "overcome" the tribe of Dan. Therefore, the "daughter of troops" in Micah 5:1 is a reference to the tribe of Gad. The name Gad means "troop" and Genesis 49:19 refers to Gad as a troop. The person that is laying siege to Israel in Micah 5:1 is the judge of Israel; as seen from Genesis: 49:16, this is the tribe of Dan. Therefore, Micah 5:1 is just repeating what we already know from Genesis 49:16–19: one day the tribe of Gad will stand up and defeat the tribe of Dan. Micah chapter 5 is a detailed description of how Gad defeats Dan. Later in this chapter, we see a description of Jesus Christ arriving on the scene to protect Israel from the Antichrist. Micah 5:5 describes how Christ (who is called "the peace" in this verse) teams up with the tribe of Gad in the form of the "seven shepherds and eight principal men" mentioned in this verse to defeat the Assyrian (the Antichrist from the tribe of Dan).

5

End-Time Summary

As I have mentioned previously in this book, most conservative theologians teach that the next prophetic event to occur is the invasion of Israel by Russia. However, if am correct and we are "living in the age of the ram and the goat," then there are many events that are yet to occur that happen prior to this invasion.

The purpose of this chapter is to summarize the observations I have made in the previous chapters and apply a potential timeline to these events. This should give the reader a bird's eye view of the prophetic calendar based on this book as well as some potential newspaper headlines to look for.

What to Look For from 2011–2020

I expect to see prophecy fulfilled in three different areas concurrently in the next few years until 2014: the withdrawal of the U.S. forces from the Persian Gulf, the rise of the democratic movement in Iran, and the selection of a Greek Secretary General of the United Nations.

You don't have to be much of a prophet to predict that the United States is going to pull its forces out of Iraq; President George W. Bush announced our withdrawal from Iraq should occur by 2011 while he was in office and President Barack Obama has also endorsed this withdrawal deadline. Neither do you have to be politically astute to predict that President Obama will probably pull the U.S. forces out of Afghanistan before the end of his presidency. What is interesting though is that Daniel's vision of the ram and the goat suggests that the U.S. is not present in the Persian Gulf. Since the military forces of the "goat" must come from the west according to Daniel chapter 8, then it seems that this vision requires that there not be a U.S. presence in the Persian Gulf area for the U.S. forces to come from the west.

While the U.S. involvement in the Persian Gulf will be winding down, the political turmoil in Iran will be ramping up. The democratic movement in Iran continues to stand up to Ahmadinejad's government over the dubious results of the election that returned him to power in June of 2009.

Daniel's description of the ram (Iran) is of a divided government led by the Persians and the Medes. The Persians represent the Iranians (and Ahmadinejad) and the Medes represent the Kurds (in their role in the democratic movement) as I described in chapter 1 of this book. The Kurds will have to arise to prominence within the Iranian government for Daniel's vision to be fulfilled.

Another event to watch for is the selection of the next Secretary General of the United Nations that will start the new term in January 2012; I believe this new Secretary General will represent the nation of Greece. The Greek secretary general of the United Nations is an important feature of the fulfillment of the "goat" as described by Daniel.

While the democratic opposition strengthens in Iran, Iran will be planning for the day the U.S. leaves the Persian Gulf (I expect this to happen near the ending of Obama's term or the beginning of the new president's term, about 2012). Even though General Petraus has announced a withdrawal no sooner than 2014, I would not be surprised to see President Obama announce a revised withdrawal date just prior to his reelection campaign in 2012. Daniel chapter 8 describes how the ram (Iran) will invade to the west (Iraq), then the north (Turkey), and then to the south (Saudi Arabia). If President Obama pulls U.S. forces from Afghanistan prior to the end of his administration, I fully expect that Iran will invade Iraq. Iraq will be so militarily weak compared to Iran that Iran should be able to blitz right through Iraq on its way to Turkey. If Iran is able to control Turkey relatively quickly, it will have a tremendous tactical advantage: the U.S. will not have a convenient location to stage its ground forces. The only location really available for a ground invasion on the Mediterranean would be in Israel, but these troops would have to travel across Lebanon and Syria to get to Turkey and Iraq. Since Lebanon and Syria are political allies of Iran this is an improbable scenario. The revolution in Egypt may adversely impact this situation. Will Egypt now allow the United States to use the Suez Canal to transport their naval forces from the Mediterranean Sea to the Red Sea to confront Iran? If not, then the only option left for the U.S. would be to send troops by ship around Africa to land in Saudi Arabia, an ally of the U.S. located next to Iraq, which would add several weeks to the response time.

While the U.S. is transporting its troops to the battle, this will give Iran time to move south and capture Saudi Arabia, thus nullifying the U.S. strategy of landing in Saudi Arabia. This would force the U.S. to conduct an aerial bombing campaign so that a landing area somewhere in the Persian Gulf for ground forces could be established. This is just the scenario that Daniel describes. Daniel notes that the "goat" (U.S. led U.N. forces) first comes across the face of the earth without touching the ground (aerial or naval forces) and then "ran unto him" (since the ram is "running" it must be now using ground forces).

It also appears from Daniel's description that the U.S. doesn't retaliate to Iran's invasion immediately. Daniel 11:2 seems to describe how Iran will use its great wealth (since it will control the world's oil supply) to control the world through diplomatic means: "...by his strength through his riches he shall stir up all against the realm of Grecia [Greece]" (the realm of Greece must be the United Nations). Iran will essentially bribe the individual members of the U.N. with cheap oil and natural gas so that the U.N. cannot establish a consensus among its nations to punish Iran. This interpretation also means that the U.S. will seek consensus with U.N. before it invades Iran, rather than going against Iran "solo."

Iran will become an exceedingly wealthy nation, since it will have plundered the petroleum resources of Iraq and Saudi Arabia. It will control the distribution of that petroleum to the west through the pipelines in Turkey. The world will tolerate this situation for only so long. Then, the U.S. will work with the U.N. to invade Iran (I expect this to happen sometime between 2015–2018). The president of Iran will be an Iranian during this time of unprecedented wealth, but a new leader in Iran will arise during the war with the U.S. and the U.N. which will be Kurdish.

The U.S. will concentrate their air assaults to allow them to take back Iraq so that the U.S. can land their ground forces there. The U.S. will invade Iran from Iraq near the Karun River as predicted by Daniel. Iran will be crushed by the U.S. invasion and dispersed to virtually every nation of the world as predicted by the prophet Jeremiah. The U.N. will probably control all the wealth of the Persian Gulf for a short period of time until an "unknown" event occurs. Daniel describes this as the great horn of the goat being "broken." I believe this is a description of tragic, catastrophic event that results in the U.S. losing its position as world's sole military superpower (this will happen about August of 2020; I'll explain why below). The U.S. in its weakened state will not be the stabilizing force in the U.N. anymore and the U.N. will break up into four regional world organizations (one for each direction: north, south, east, and west).

When Will the U.S. Military Become "Broken"?

Why do I believe the U.S. will cease to be the world's sole military superpower in August of 2020? Here is my rationale:

As I mentioned earlier in this book, I believe that the relationship of the U.S. and Iraq represents Daniel's first "beast": the lion with eagle's wings. Daniel describes how this beast will lose its wings (representing the downfall of the U.S. military) and then later stand up like a man (a description of the rise of the Antichrist and the rise of Babylon in Iraq). This description is remarkably similar to the life of Nebuchadnezzar when he went insane for a period of seven years. Daniel describes how his fingernails looked like "eagle talons" and his hair appeared as "feathers" during this period. If these two descriptions can be linked together then it appears that God is trying to say that there is a period of seven years between when the U.S. falls as a world military power and the Antichrist rises in the middle of the tribulational period. If this analysis is viable, I think I can firmly date the time when the U.S. is "broken." The reason I can do this is because I think the Bible provides us evidence of when the midpoint of the tribulational period occurs.

When I was writing my book, *The Fourth Day: Why the Bible is Historically Accurate* (Raleigh, NC: Lulu Publishers, 2006 [ISBN 9781430310624]), I was trying to show that the dating of Old Testament history as described in the Bible was different than what was being proposed by secular historians. I was looking for astronomical evidence in the Old Testament that would be useful in dating the events of the Babylonian Captivity of Judah. I was able to find such a description in Jeremiah 15:9, "She that hath borne seven languisheth: she hath given up the ghost; her sun is gone down while it was yet day…" How did I decide this was a description of the sky? I had to ask this question: What kind of woman has her own sun? Certainly no flesh-and-blood person. Yet, suppose this verse was metaphorically speaking of a woman in the sky: the constellation Virgo. If "the sun is gone down while it is yet day," couldn't this be the description of a solar eclipse? I was able to find a solar eclipse that occurred over Israel on August 14, 393 BC that fits this verse very well. This was an annular eclipse where Virgo was located in the middle of the sky with seven bodies (sun and moon with five planets) forming a line to Virgo's "womb." Doesn't this fit Jeremiah's description of the woman who has "born seven" in this verse?

I believe there was another description of this solar eclipse in another verse (Jeremiah 6:4–5): "Prepare ye war against her; arise, and let us go up at noon. Woe unto us! For the day goeth away, for the shadows of the evening are stretched out. Arise, and let us go by night, and let us destroy her palaces."

This verse describes the events involved in Nebuchadnezzar's invasion of Israel to destroy Jerusalem and Solomon's Temple. Many theologians interpret this verse as saying that Nebuchadnezzar's forces have waited too long to invade during the day, so they wait to invade during the night. Why didn't they just wait to invade during the next day? It is certainly easier for them to fight during the day. I think something else is happening here. What is interesting in this verse is the over-reaction of Nebuchadnezzar's forces to the sun going down: "Woe unto us!" Suppose this wasn't an overreaction? If this verse is a description of a solar eclipse their response makes perfect sense. The Babylonians worshipped the celestial bodies so a solar eclipse could very well be a good reason to alter a military invasion: it could be a sign these gods were unhappy with what you were doing. Thales of Miletus tells the account of a war between Lydia and Media in which a solar eclipse occurred very near the same period of history; the two armies ceased all fighting and signed a peace treaty because they feared they had angered the celestial gods. It appears that the Babylonian's interpretation of the solar eclipse was that the celestial gods didn't want them to invade during the day but rather at night (when a solar eclipse could not occur). Also notice what the Babylonians don't say; they don't say that it became dark in the middle of the day. If it did this would be evidence of full solar eclipse but since this was an annular eclipse that wouldn't happen. The eclipse would occur but it wouldn't go completely dark. The Babylonians do mention something that happens in any solar eclipse (including an annular eclipse). Note that they say that the "shadows of the evening were stretched out" (literally the shadows were distorted). Even an annular solar eclipse causes strange appearances in shadows; they can appear to race along the ground and take on distorted outlines.

Since I was able to find this solar eclipse in the book of Jeremiah, I then wondered if there were other astronomical descriptions in the Bible. Upon looking further, I found two others in the book of Revelation in chapter 12. Let's look at the first astronomical description; consider Revelation 12:3–4: "And there appeared another wonder in heaven; and behold a great red dragon, having seven heads and ten horns, and seven crowns upon his heads. And his tail drew the third part of the stars of heaven…"

If this describes another solar eclipse, when do I look for it? I believe that there are seven thousand years that will pass from the first day of creation to the last day of the millennial kingdom of Christ. The events of the tribulational period happen one thousand years before the end of the millennial period, or six thousand years after the first day of creation. I showed in my book, *The Fourth Day: Why the Bible is Historically Accurate*, that four thousand years elapsed from the first day of creation until the crucifixion of Jesus Christ. Since Christ was crucified about 31 AD, then we should expect the tribulational period to occur very near 2031 AD. I was able to find a solar eclipse that appears to be a good fit for the verses in Revelation (Revelation 12:3–4), that will take place over Israel on August 2, 2027 AD. The constellation Hydra (the water serpent) will have its head in the center of the sky, located just below the constellation Cancer. Seven bodies (sun, moon, and five planets) will be spread across the sky along the elliptic line through the constellation Cancer from east to west. These seven bodies could represent the seven heads of the dragon in these verses. The constellation Hydra is the largest of all the constellations, so it could be considered "great" like the dragon is described in Revelation 12:3.

The other astronomical description is described in Revelation 12:1: "And there appeared a great wonder in heaven; a woman clothed with the sun, and the moon under her feet, and upon her head a crown of twelve stars." I believe this is a description of the sky in Israel at sunset on August 5, 2027 AD. The constellation Virgo will be seen on the western horizon at sunset (standing on her head), and a new moon (slightly crescent moon) will be located by Virgo's head.

Since this will happen at sunset, the sky will be "clothed in the sun" and since Virgo is standing on its head, the moon will be located below its feet in the sky. The fascinating aspect of this discovery is that these astronomical signs are separated by a period of three days. The context of the reading of Revelation chapter 12 certainly causes the reader to believe these events would be very close to one another in time.

The Timeline from 2020–2024

It will be the year 2020 after the U.S. is broken, Iran is dispersed across the world, and the U.N. is divided into four world powers. I believe the four world powers of the former U.N. are described in the Bible by their directions (north, south, east, and west) and they become the next prominent world powers. The military struggle between the north (led by Russia) and the south (led by Egypt) dominates world events as described in Daniel chapter 11 starting with verse 5. An attempt to coordinate a treaty between the north and the south is carried out by the daughter of the king of the south. However, it appears that the king of the north tricks the south and the treaty is to no avail. The south then seeks revenge and invades the north and is able to bring back prominent leaders captive and spoil the north. The invasions go back and forth between the north and the south three more times until the north (Russia) invades the glorious land (Israel). This invasion is described in Daniel 11:15–17. I believe this is the same invasion that is described in Ezekiel chapters 38 and 39, the invasion of Gog (Russia) into Israel. Some conservative theologians believe that this invasion occurs about seven months prior to the beginning of the tribulational period (I believe the tribulational period begins in 2024). This is based on two descriptions in these two chapters in Ezekiel: it will take seven months to bury the bodies of the Russian forces destroyed by God and it will take seven years to burn up all the military supplies left by Russians for fuel in Israel (these seven years coincide with the tribulational period). (If there are only seven months from Russia's invasion until the beginning of the tribulational period, then these seven months are described in Daniel 11:18–20.)

Next, the king of Russia invades the isles (possibly the nations in the Mediterranean Sea) and then returns to his own land where he disappears. His successor is mentioned in Daniel 11:20. His is not the military leader that the former ruler was; he is content to be a "raiser of taxes" in "the glory of the kingdom." Russia is very rich at this point and this ruler's intention is to invest the spoils of war into monuments that declare the might of the powerful nation of Russia to the world. However, the reign of this ruler is short. Daniel 11:20 states that his reign is only a matter of days. How many days? I think the Bible tells us.

The length of this ruler's reign is a prophetic sign because his successor is the Antichrist (Isaiah 23:15): "And it shall come to pass in that day, that Tyre shall be forgotten seventy years, according to the days of one king: after the end of seventy years shall Tyre sing as a harlot." The word "days" used here is commonly used in the Hebrew to describe literal, twenty-four-hour days. Therefore, I believe this verse is best interpreted as saying that Tyre will be forgotten for seventy years and this king with the short reign only rules for seventy days. Therefore this seventy year period that Tyre has been forgotten has to have been taking place during our lifetime. So, when did this seventy year period start?

Before you can be "forgotten," you have to be remembered.

Shortly after World War II, the United Nations authored an agreement that would protect archaeological and cultural sites from destruction due to acts of war. Nations that sign this treaty agree not to aim their weapons at the protected sites, and also not to hide behind such sites during times of war. The agreement is called the "1954 Hague Convention for the Protection of Cultural Property in the Event of Armed Conflict." There is a large sign located in Lebanon that states that the "ancient" city of Tyre is protected by the U.N. by this treaty. I believe that this treaty signifies the beginning of this seventy year period which began in 1954 and will end in 2024.

There is a city of Tyre that is on the mainland of Lebanon, but the "ancient" city of Tyre was actually an island located near the coastline. Alexander the Great's invasion of Tyre involved the construction of a causeway (a "pathway" built of rocks used to access Tyre from the shore). The causeway still exists and has expanded some over the years from the buildup of silt. It is the ancient city of Tyre that will be rebuilt by the Antichrist. He will use Tyre as his base for his worldwide religion (Isaiah 23:17): "And it shall come to pass after the end of seventy years, that the Lord will visit Tyre, and she shall turn to her hire, and shall commit fornication with all the kingdoms of the world upon the face of the earth."

Tyre will also be a market that will solely be in the business of providing supplies for the new Temple in Israel (Isaiah 23:18): "And her merchandise and her hire shall be holiness to the Lord: it shall not be treasured nor laid up; for her merchandise shall be for them that dwell before the Lord, to eat sufficiently, and for durable clothing."

The Timeline from 2024–2031

This is the seven year tribulational period. The Antichrist will rise with a small people: the Kurds and the Assyrians. Daniel 11:21–45 describes the exploits of the Antichrist from the beginning of the tribulational period (2024) to its midpoint (August 2027). The beginning of Daniel chapter 12 describes how the angel Michael will deliver the people found written in the book. Those that love God during this period will be taken up to heaven. This occurs at the midpoint of the tribulational period. Those that remain will be the followers of the Antichrist. We are not given many details from the midpoint to the end of the tribulational period, since Daniel is told to "shut up the words and seal the book."

6

Why Is All This Important?

The purpose of this book is to demonstrate to the reader that we no longer have to wait for the fulfillment of end-time prophecy; we are just starting to enter into the age of fulfilled prophecy. We are *Living in the Age of the Ram and the Goat*. So, if I have convinced you that this is true, what should you do?

The study of prophecy in the Bible is always a call to act righteously, pleasing God in the way we live (1 Timothy 4:1–4):

> Now the Spirit speaketh expressly, that in the latter times some shall depart from the faith, giving heed to seducing spirits, and doctrines of devils. Speaking lies in hypocrisy; having their conscience seared with a hot iron. Forbidding to marry, and commanding to abstain from meats, which God hath created to be received with thanksgiving of them which believe and know the truth. For every creature of God is good, and nothing

to be refused, if it be received with thanksgiving: For it is sanctified by the word of God and prayer.

Timothy is stating here that during the end times there would be some who abandon faith in Christ. They would act as lying hypocrites having their consciences seared; they will lose their desire to say "no" to abominable behavior. This future society will forbid marriage. (We have already seen attempts in our society where marriage is being devalued by allowing people to marry any "thing," including inanimate objects. Several examples can be found on the Web, but one of the more disturbing instances is the woman who "married" the Eiffel Tower. Seriously. There was a ceremony, and she changed her last name to "Eiffel," and then went on to become founder of the "OS Internationale," an educational website and community for those also suffering from a serious romantic interest in inanimate objects. There is even a medical and scientific term for this sinful behavior: objectum sexuality [objectophilia]. Here's the official internet article: The Independent, "I Married the Eiffel Tower," May 25, 2008; http://www.independent.co.uk/extras/sunday-review/living/i-married-the-eiffel-tower-832519.html.) This future society will forbid eating meat (much like animal rights activists are trying to impose on our society now). Timothy is warning us that as we approach the end times, our society is going to deteriorate morally to the extent that we will be unable to distinguish between righteousness and debauchery.

If you are a Christian, you need to repent. Turn away from behavior that the Bible makes clear is wrong. Aspire to behave like a prophet. Stand up against the sinful acts of our society that the world calls "normal." Jesus called us His prophets (Matthew 5: 11–12): "Blessed are ye, when men shall revile you, and persecute you, and shall say all manner of evil against you falsely, for my sake. Rejoice, and be exceeding glad: for great is your reward in heaven: for so persecuted they the prophets before you." The apostle Peter also referred to us as "the children of the prophets," those that will stand up in our world for righteousness (Acts 3:25): "Ye are the children of the prophets, and of the covenant which God made with our fathers, saying unto Abraham, And in thy seed shall all the kindreds of the earth be blessed."

If you believe that the world is coming to an end and you don't already know Jesus Christ as your Lord and Savior, you should soberly seek Him today. As you can see from this book, God is active and intimately involved in the events of your life; He wants to redeem you so that you can experience a better life. A life devoted to Him.